Speedbuilder
Second Edition

Bryan Coombs

Pitman

PITMAN PUBLISHING LIMITED
128 Long Acre, London WC2E 9AN

Associated Companies
Pitman Publishing Pty Ltd, Melbourne
Pitman Publishing New Zealand Ltd, Wellington

© Pitman Publishing Limited 1983

First edition 1976
Second edition 1983
Reprinted 1984

Text set in 11/12pt IBM Baskerville,
printed and bound in Great Britain
at The Pitman Press, Bath

ISBN 0 273 01956 2

CONTENTS

PREFACE

The aim of the book is to improve speed through a series of drills and exercises, with a concentration on speed reading.

Two units in each chapter revise short forms, intersections and phrases; complete mastery of these outlines is essential to speed. A correspondence unit provides additional practice material for the short forms, intersections and phrases. Unit C contains the only long passage, which gives general and specific information about shorthand writing, and provides further dictation material. Points of technique in the skill of shorthand writing are discussed and illustrated in Unit E which appears in chapters one to ten only.

Reading for speed is an activity which has not been stressed nearly enough. Shorthand writers should be able to read shorthand *at least* 50 per cent faster than they can write it. Striving to read shorthand rapidly with fluency and confidence will, automatically, be reflected in one's writing ability.

All rapid reading drills must be followed by dictation of those drills. After preparing the drills the dictation speed should be some 20 w.p.m. above one's ordinary rate of writing. The student now writing at 80 w.p.m., or who is preparing for an examination at that speed, should aim to read the material at a speed of at least 120 w.p.m. and take dictation of that prepared material at 100 w.p.m.

Speedbuilder has a companion edition in Pitman New Era Shorthand. This should prove to be useful in speed classes for Pitman 2000 and Pitman New Era Shorthand writers.

Bryan Coombs
Chartered Shorthand Reporter
Senior Lecturer in Secretarial Studies
Newcastle upon Tyne Polytechnic

CHAPTER 1

Unit A—Short Forms and Derivatives

Drill the following:

a/an   accord/according/according to   accordingly   all   almost

although   always   also   and   are   as/has   ought   be

yesterday   together   being

1. Read through the following passage, noting how long it takes you.
   If you cannot read any outline check the key.

   > Time . . . . . . mins . . . . . . secs

2. Repeat the reading exercise, aiming to increase your reading speed.
   Note your timing.

   > Time . . . . . . mins . . . . . . secs

3. Drill all outlines which caused you any hesitancy in the last reading.
   Now repeat the reading, aiming to read the shorthand as quickly as
   if the material was typewritten. This final reading should be followed
   by dictation of the passage.

   > Time . . . . . . mins . . . . . . secs

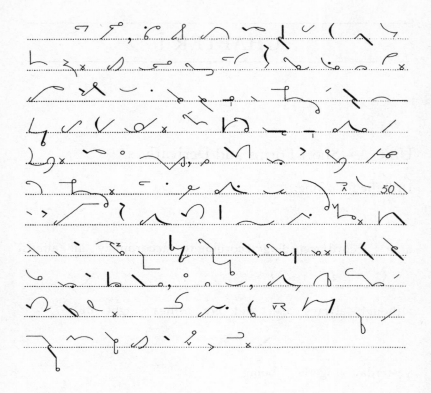

According to the records, sales yesterday were almost double what/they should be for the time of the year. We/shall increase production accordingly although the present phase may not/last. We must always be in a position to supply/goods to customers and be able to make changes when/they are necessary. Prompt deliveries together with good service are/ essential. Almost as important, is the ability to meet all/the special requests from customers. According to a recent survey/ new orders account for 50% of all the/work although we have also had many repeat items. It/will be up to all employees to take advantage of/the opportunities being presented to us. It ought to be/possible for us to meet all demands because, as you/know, we have the latest equipment and also the best/ staff. Occasionally we need this kind of challenge to test/our capabilities and I am positive we shall all rise/to the occasion.

(163)

Unit B—Phrasing

The doubling principle is used in phrasing for the addition of there/their, dear, other and order.

1. Read through the shorthand passage, noting how long it takes you. If you cannot read any outline encircle it in pencil and check it in the key.

Time . . . . . . mins . . . . . . secs

2. Drill all outlines encircled in pencil. Repeat the reading, aiming for an increased reading speed.

Time . . . . . . mins . . . . . . secs

3. Make a fair copy of the passage in your own notebook. Look at the shorthand material, absorb several outlines and then make your own notes without reference to the printed passage. At first you might be able to recall only one complete outline to transfer to your own notes, but with practice you will be able to write several outlines, or a short sentence, without referring to the passage.

4. Now a final reading before receiving the passage from dictation. The aim is to read RAPIDLY.

Time . . . . . . mins . . . . . . secs

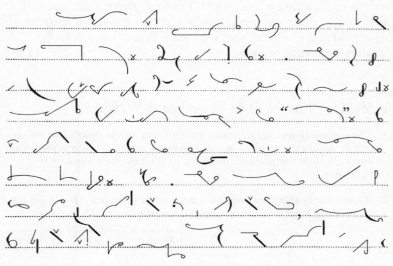

3

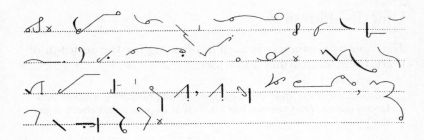

In order that we may write quickly it is essential/that we look at the subject in the correct order./There is no other way of doing this. The experts/say that students should have their theory completely within their/command and yet for some reason or other many students/do not. In other words they are unaware for example/of the phrase "my dear sir". This might well be/because this phrase is no longer very common. In some/other place at some other time it was. On the/other hand the experts in their opinion further state that/most rules do not have to be learned by heart/but rather by application, and in their view this is/achieved by writing outlines many times in order that they/can be recalled and written without hesitation. This works for/some people but in some other cases students still have/difficulty in making their way and some other means of/learning is necessary. I believe there is far too little/work done on speed reading, reading printed shorthand as quickly/as possible, and I am sure there is much to/be gained by this approach. (195)

Unit C—The Skill of Shorthand Writing

1. The following passage contains information about shorthand writing which should prove to be useful to you as a student shorthand writer. Read through the passage, referring to the key for assistance if necessary.

2. Repeat the reading, noting the time it takes and encircling in pencil any outline which causes hesitancy in reading.

Time . . . . . . mins . . . . . . secs

3. Drill the outlines which caused hesitancy. How many times you drill is a very individual thing. Write the outline several, or many, times (repeating it to yourself as you write) until you feel you have it under your control. Now make a final reading of the passage, noting your time, which should show a marked improvement on the first timing, in preparation for receiving the passage from dictation.

Time . . . . . . mins . . . . . . secs

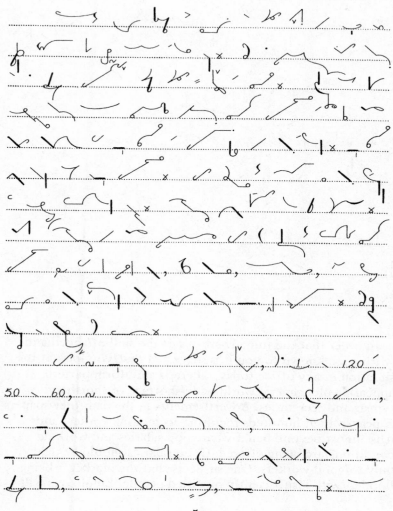

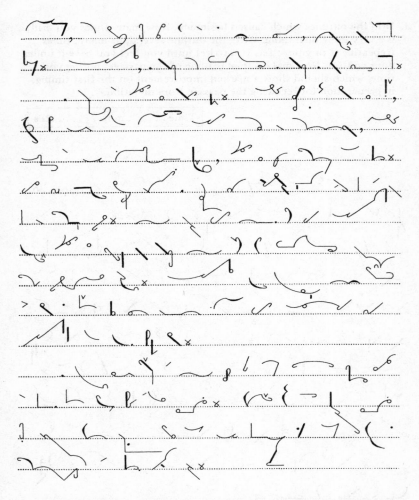

In order that the full advantages of the skill of/shorthand
writing are known to you it is suggested that/you look at the
situation in any office today. There/is a uniform pattern
appearing of a general world-wide/shortage of shorthand-
typists and secretaries. Advertisements in the daily/newspapers
appear in their hundreds requiring secretarial workers and
it/is almost beyond belief what good salaries and working
conditions/are being offered. Good salaries should be paid
only to/good workers. One suspects that the market is being
flooded/with insufficiently qualified people. Employers will

be tolerant for just/so long. Already employers are almost unanimous when they declare/that the quality of the secretarial worker is not what/it used to be, and this is because, in their/opinion, not sufficient skill is being acquired by the individual/before going out to work. There is considerable evidence to/substantiate their claim.

When you have good speeds in shorthand/and typewriting, say 100 to 120 and 50/to 60, you have two basic skills which will enable/you to travel the world, with a good job at/any place you care to stop, or an entry into/a good secretarial post in your own country. These skills/should be supported by a good general education, with particular/emphasis on English, together with office practice. Another language, or/specialist training such as that of a medical secretary, will/be found to be of great advantage. In other words,/the better your qualifications the better the job you can/get.

The potential of shorthand is beyond doubt. In spite/of the suggestions that the subject is dying, and this/has been said now for longer than anyone cares to/remember, and in spite of the introduction of new electronic/devices, shorthand is still very much in demand. Once you/have given sufficient attention to learning the system you will/always be able to call upon it and put it/to very good use. Many people when making their way/in the world have found shorthand has proved to be/better than many of their other qualifications purely from the/usefulness point of view. In other words even if there/is no immediate application of the subject a time does/seem to come along when in some other way you/are rewarded for having studied the subject.

The future is/now bright and many students achieve much more than their/dreams as a result of taking time over the study/of the office skills. They will find that they can/depend upon their skills training to prepare them to take/their place in the new technological age in which they/have a very important and demanding role to play. (459)

Unit D—Correspondence

1. Read through the following two passages, referring to the key if necessary. Note carefully the outlines for towns and countries which may be new to you.

7

2. Drill any outlines new to you. Make a fair copy of each letter. Repeat the reading of each letter, noting the time.

> Time . . . . . . mins . . . . . . secs

3. Finally, repeat the reading. Aim to read *at least* 30 to 40 words a minute faster than your writing speed, which means that everyone should be reading at a rate of at least 100 words a minute. Note the time taken.

> Time . . . . . . mins . . . . . . secs

Letter A

8

Letter B

8050., ..., usa

358.,

Letter A

To: The Managing Director, Wonder Products, Central
         Avenue, London SW/3 4AF
From: Alexander Jackson, Sales Manager, Jackson
         Electronics/Limited, 75 Central Avenue, Hobart,
         Tasmania.
Dear Sir,
      This/letter is to introduce to you a new range of/products

which have not yet been seen in your country./Agents have
been interviewed and appointed in the Common Market/
countries and they are all unanimous about the outstanding
future/our products will have in their countries. According
to them,/sales have been beyond belief.

The enclosed catalogue gives full/details together with
prices and discounts. In order that you/may take full advantage
of the discounts offered for bulk/orders we are reducing the
minimum figures set out in/the catalogue by 50% for your
first order./

All orders receive prompt attention because it is our
belief/that first-class service is essential in this age of/speed.
Any complaints are given a sympathetic and full investigation./

I look forward to hearing from you. Even if you/do not
place an order immediately I would be thankful/to have your
opinion on the products we manufacture.

Yours/faithfully,   (191)

Letter B

To: The Manager, Sanderson Precision Instruments Limited,
        North Road, Birmingham, England./
From : The Production Manager, Henderson Aircraft
        Corporation, P.O. Box 8/050, Seattle, U.S.A.

Dear Sir,

Our/order for fuel gauges, 100 of model 35/8, was received
yesterday. Unfortunately ten of the instruments have/been
damaged in transit, and I suspect that this was/largely due to
faulty packing of the one case which/contained all of the ten.

These goods are now on/their way back to you. Would
you please credit our/account or send me a revised statement
giving the balance/now due.

I am sure you will appreciate that all/goods in transit are
subject to many stresses and strains/and that exceptional
care is necessary when packing equipment for/long journeys.
To help you in any insurance claim involved,/and to
substantiate my claim, I am also returning the/packing case.
This may help establish where the fault lies./

If you need to contact me urgently about this matter/
please use my telegraphic address.

Yours faithfully,   (177)

Unit E—Technique

Turning the Page

Page turning occurs frequently during each session of dictation. It must be completed with ease and speed. It may seem a trivial thing to consider, but it involves time, and time is all important during dictation.

The steps illustrated below are for a right-handed writer:

The page has a margin, and the first page of each day is dated. Before beginning to write take hold of the bottom left-hand corner of the page with finger and thumb. Allow the page to lie completely flat except for that tiny corner which you are holding.

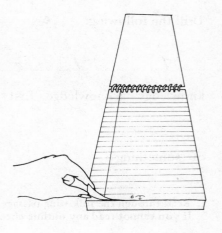

Start writing on the top line and continue doing so, filling each line, until the page is filled.

As the last line is filled quickly turn (flick) the page over.

Start writing on the first line of the next page.

Without looking, let your left hand feel its way down the page immediately, and take hold of the left-hand corner. You now know that you are ready for the next page turning.

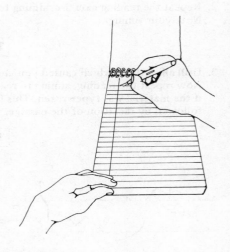

Again, keep the page flat, fill all the lines and as the last line is completed quickly flick the page over.

CHAPTER 2

Unit A—Short Forms and Derivatives

Drill the following:

knowledge   acknowledge   first   had/dollar   large   more

of   something

1. Read through the following passage, noting how long it takes you.
   If you cannot read any outline check the key.

Time . . . . . . mins . . . . . . secs

2. Repeat the reading exercise, aiming to increase your reading speed.
   Note your timing.

Time . . . . . . mins . . . . . . secs

3. Drill all outlines which caused you any hesitancy in the last reading.
   Now repeat the reading, aiming to read the shorthand as quickly as
   if the material was typewritten. This final reading should be
   followed by dictation of the passage.

Time . . . . . . mins . . . . . . secs

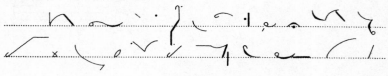

12

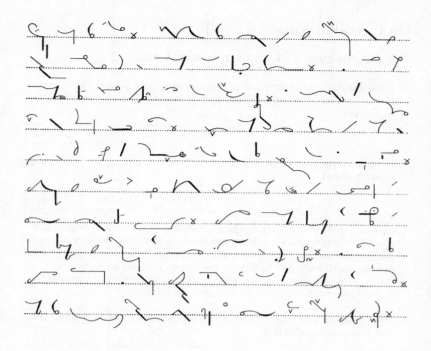

It will be something of a tragedy if more aid/is not made available for this work. After the first/appeal we acknowledged every single letter which flooded into this/office. I believe this must be our first priority because/the public expects us to acknowledge any donation they make./The cost of such acknowledgements does of course reduce the/amount for final distribution. A number of large firms might/be asked to give more. To my knowledge most of/them are only too willing to assist and such large/organizations often have dollars to spare for a good cause./We have had the first sign of the cuts which/ will be necessary unless funds are increased and something must/be done quickly. We must acknowledge the danger that exists/and take advantage of the first opportunity that comes along/to ease the situation. The more dollars we can collect/ the better we shall be able to cope with any/large emergency that occurs. Knowledge of this financial problem should/be treated as something quite private within the society.   (179)

Unit B—Phrasing

Halving principle — it, to, not, would, time.

1. Read through the shorthand passage, noting how long it takes you. If you cannot read any outline encircle it with a pencil and check it in the key.

   Time . . . . . . mins . . . . . . secs

2. Drill all outlines encircled. Repeat the reading, aiming for an increased reading speed.

   Time . . . . . . mins . . . . . . secs

3. Make a fair copy of the passage in your own notebook. Look at the shorthand material, absorb several outlines and then make your own notes without reference to the printed passage. At first you might be able to recall only one complete outline to transfer to your own notes, but with practice you will be able to write several outlines, or a short sentence, without referring to the passage.

4. Now a final reading before receiving the passage from dictation. The aim is to read RAPIDLY.

   Time . . . . . . mins . . . . . . secs

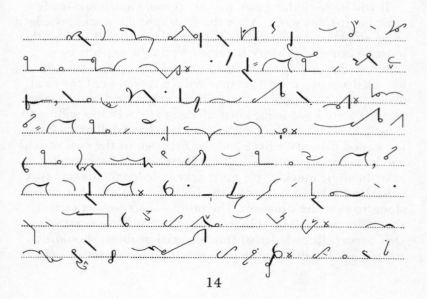

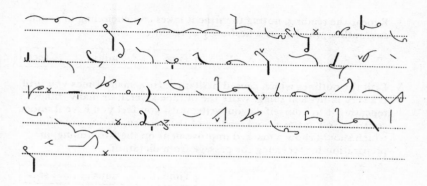

You will not be so very much surprised to be/told that the difference in size of shorthand strokes is/extremely important. A large double-length stroke should always be/quite distinct, because if it is not there will be/a danger of many words being misread. At the same/time half-length strokes should stand out clearly in your/notes. In other words write these strokes so that you/will not be in any doubt as to whether any/stroke is ordinary length, half length or double length. This/is a good general rule and it would be something/of a pity to neglect this point when revising any/part of the theory. Immediate improvement has been found by/students in all parts of the world when using this/suggestion. One is able to achieve maximum speed in the/minimum of time if you have complete confidence. You will/not advance if you do not take care over the/size of your notes and have some pride in your/general style of outlines. Good shorthand is easier and faster/to transcribe, which is something rather important for you to/remember. There is no point in writing shorthand if you/cannot at all times transcribe at speed and with accuracy./

(210)

Unit C—The Skill of Shorthand Writing

1. The following passage contains information about shorthand writing which should prove useful to you as a student shorthand writer. Read through the passage, referring to the key for assistance if necessary.

15

2. Repeat the reading, noting the time it takes and encircling in pencil any outline which causes hesitancy in reading.

> Time . . . . . . mins . . . . . . secs

3. Drill the outlines which caused hesitancy. How many times you drill is a very individual thing. Write the outline several, or many, times repeating it to yourself as you write, until you feel you have it under control. Now make a final reading of the passage, noting your time, which should show a marked improvement on the first timing, in preparation for receiving the passage from dictation.

> Time . . . . . . mins . . . . . . secs

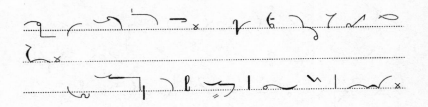

You will not make very much progress in the study/of
shorthand if your general knowledge of English is not/
something rather above average. Shorthand is a linguistic skill
and/in the study of any language it is essential to/come to
grips with the meanings and spellings of words/and to have a
thorough understanding of the basic grammar./

All shorthand notes are written for immediate or eventual
transcription/and if you are unable to read any outline you/
are not doing your job properly. Employers want an
efficient/and capable shorthand-typist, or secretary, one
who can take/dictation and from her notes produce a piece
of mailable/work, which the dictator can merely glance at
and sign/with confidence. The dictator has his own work
to do/within the organization and he is not paid to check/
through your work for errors — that is your job.

Nobody,/absolutely nobody, can become an efficient
shorthand writer with a/poor knowledge of the language
they are using, which in/our case is English. There are many
so-called shorthand-/typists and secretaries holding jobs
right now by the skin/of their teeth, but they are not
worthy of earning/the salaries they receive because their
productivity is so low,/and it is only because of the present
shortage of/secretarial workers that such people are being
employed at all./They would not be employable if there
was a surplus/of shorthand-typists. This present state of
affairs cannot last/for ever and soon there will be a real
danger/for anyone entering this work without maximum
English qualifications.

Let/us be perfectly clear. No employer is complaining
about shorthand/speeds or typewriting speeds, only English.
If you are prepared/to acknowledge the fact that this

18

subject is not your/strongest you are then advised to take immediate steps to/overcome this weakness. I do not think it is necessary/for anyone to go and take a formal course of/English at a college, unless there is a marked deficiency,/ but a quick working through of a standard English textbook/ would be a good revision. English knowledge will automatically improve/with a daily reading of one of the national newspapers;/the meanings of any words not understood should be checked/immediately. If you refer to a dictionary which also has/shorthand outlines as well as meanings you will be doing/two important jobs at the same time. The reading of/at least one book a month from the library should/be a definite aim; this will expand your general knowledge/and widen your vocabulary.

Familiar words are easier to take/in shorthand and easier to transcribe. Become familiar with as/many words as you possibly can. Words are your raw/material.

Whenever you make a mistake in a shorthand outline,/or whenever you make a spelling mistake, it is essential/that you take remedial action so that the same mistake/will never occur again. Drill those errors until you are/the master of them.

If you have neglected your study/of English do something about it immediately.

(517)

Unit D—Correspondence

1. Read through the following two passages, referring to the key if necessary. Note carefully the outlines for towns and countries which may be new to you.

2. Drill any outlines new to you. Make a fair copy of each letter. Repeat the reading of each letter, noting the time.

Time . . . . . . mins . . . . . . secs

3. Finally, repeat the reading. Aim to read *at least* 30 to 40 words a minute faster than your writing speed, which means that everyone should be reading at a rate of at least 100 words a minute. Note the time taken.

Time . . . . . . mins . . . . . . secs

Letter A

Letter A

To: Mr Donald Scott, 14 Bloomsbury Square, London WC1/
From: The Manager, Security & Trust Co. Ltd., 145/Regent
      Street, London W1

Dear Sir,

   I wrote to/you two weeks ago about your neglect
concerning repayment of/the loan, and I requested that you
at least acknowledge/my communication. I am sorry not to
have received any/response from you.

In order to avoid handing over the/matter to our solicitors, with the strong possibility of a/court case following, I am once again asking you to/take immediate action about this outstanding amount owing to prevent/any unpleasantness. You will not be surprised to be told/that the amount due immediately is £100 and/I am asking you to send me your cheque for/this sum today. This would be the simplest way of/settling this matter. I would be prepared, however, to accept/a cheque for £50 now together with a postdated/ cheque for next month for the other £50.

Please/do not delay any further and do something about this/matter immediately rather than force me to take the only/alternative step.

Yours faithfully, (194)

Letter B

To: The Advertising Manager, Daily Telegraph, Fleet
        Street, London EC/4
From: Miss Ann Simpson, Managing Director, New Fashions
        Limited, 9/Albert Street, Melbourne, Australia.

Dear Sir,

I am enclosing a/draft layout for an advertisement to be placed in your/paper. I would prefer it to appear on the fashion/page rather than in the usual "situations" columns. I would/also appreciate it if your very capable display staff would/do something with the material to give the maximum effect./In other words let your staff have a free hand;/I am not at all concerned about cost. What is/most important is that I have a good response to/the advertisement from which I can make a satisfactory appointment./I have advertised for staff in newspapers in all parts/of the world but I have found that I have/been more successful in English publications than in any others./

If it is possible I would like this material to/appear within a week of receiving this letter. I am/familiar with the problems this request might cause, but it/is important to have immediate action.

Yours faithfully, (188)

Unit E—Technique

Using the Margin

Most notebooks are printed with a left-hand margin. Draw one on each page if it has not been printed.

In the early stages of learning shorthand the margin will be mainly used by the teacher for corrections.

Once you have started taking dictation at school or college and, more particularly, in the office use the margin as follows:

(a) if you do not hear something, or are unsure of a word write the outline for "ask" in the margin of the line where the query occurs;

(b) if you are not certain about a figure quoted, or an address, but you know there will be a file for you to refer to after the dictation is completed write the outline for "check" in the margin.

When dictation of that passage is completed you can quickly refer the dictator to any query you have, which is where the "ask" mark appears. Before commencing transcription you can obtain any information you require for the points marked "check".

CHAPTER 3

Unit A—Short Forms and Derivatives

Drill the following:

altogether   commercial/ly   difficult   do   has   have   having

how   information   largely   satisfaction   their/there

influential

1. Read through the following passage, noting how long it takes you.
   If you cannot read any outline check the key.

   | Time . . . . . . mins . . . . . . secs |

2. Repeat the reading exercise, aiming to increase your reading speed.
   Note your timing.

   | Time . . . . . . mins . . . . . . secs |

3. Drill all outlines which caused you any hesitancy in the last reading.
   Now repeat the reading, aiming to read the shorthand as quickly as
   if the material was typewritten. This final reading should be
   followed by dictation of the passage.

   | Time . . . . . . mins . . . . . . secs |

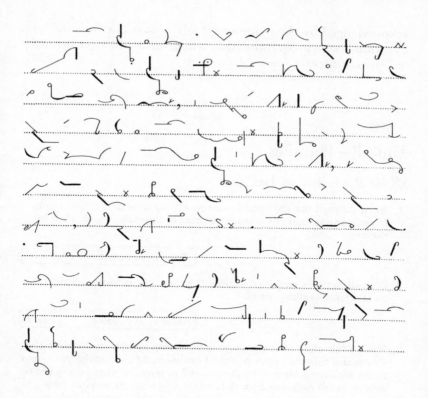

Commercial advertising is so much a part of modern life/
that it would be difficult to imagine how the world/would
be if advertisements did not exist. Commercial television has/
largely taken over as the strongest influential medium, but
newspapers/and radio do still supply information to the
public and/much of this is commercially financed. It is difficult at/times to see the entertainment value of the material
which/accompanies advertisements on television and radio,
but the sponsors are/not altogether to blame. Satisfaction
has to be given or/the members of the public would switch
off, so there/can be little cause for complaint. The commercial programmes are/having a great success and their audience
figures are altogether/admirable. Their achievements have
been largely influential in certain government/stations changing their ideas on how to satisfy the public./There is little
information on exactly how we are entertained/but it is largely

acknowledged by the commercial advertisers that/it is difficult to produce one programme that will give/satisfaction throughout the country. (174)

Unit B—Phrasing

Circle S — is, his, as, has, us.

1. Read through the shorthand passage, noting how long it takes you. If you cannot read any outline encircle it in pencil and check it in the key.

Time . . . . . . mins . . . . . . secs

2. Drill all outlines encircled in pencil. Repeat the reading, aiming for an increased reading speed.

Time . . . . . . mins . . . . . . secs

3. Make a fair copy of the passage in your own notebook. Look at the shorthand material, absorb several outlines and then make your own notes without reference to the printed passage. At first you might be able to recall only one complete outline to transfer to your own notes, but with practice you will be able to write several outlines, or a short sentence, without referring to the passage.

4. Now a final reading before receiving the passage from dictation. The aim is to read RAPIDLY.

Time . . . . . . mins . . . . . . secs

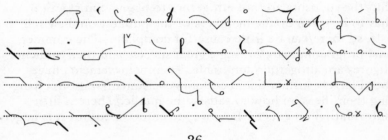

26

We can say that phrasing is just as important as/anything else within the system and it has to be/given an equal time for study because of this importance./Phrasing is often kept to the minimum because opportunities to/phrase are not taken. It is important to remember to/keep several words behind a speaker to be able to/hear and appreciate a phrase. This should be done as/early as possible in your training. If this is not/done and you write each word as it is spoken/you will simply never have the pleasure and satisfaction of/phrasing. Another point for us all to remember is that/there are quite enough phrases already in existence without more/of us creating new ones, unless they are very good/and based upon the principles of the system. Your performance/as a shorthand writer will show a marked improvement if/you have an enthusiastic appreciation for phrasing. This matter is/worthy of your attention as soon as possible if you/are not already phrasing, and it would be just as/well to start immediately if you wish to write as/fast as most people can speak. This is possible for/shorthand writers to achieve. (204)

Unit C—The Skill of Shorthand Writing

1. The following passage contains information about shorthand writing which should prove to be useful to you as a student shorthand writer. Read through the passage, referring to the key for assistance if necessary.

2. Repeat the reading, noting the time it takes and encircling in pencil any outline which causes hesitancy in reading.

Time . . . . . . mins . . . . . . secs

3. Drill the outlines which caused hesitancy. How many times you drill is a very individual thing. Write the outline several, or many, times (repeating it to yourself as you write) until you feel you have it under your control. Now make a final reading of the passage, noting your time, which should show a marked improvement on the first timing, in preparation for receiving the passage from dictation.

Time . . . . . . mins . . . . . . secs

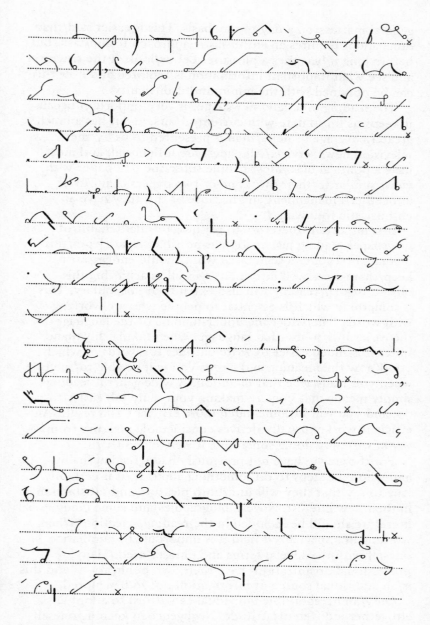

A good secretary is well-informed and she should take/every
opportunity to gather information about commercial and

general matters/on a day-to-day basis. This is easier said/than done and it requires an enthusiastic approach to the/task, but before long it becomes a pleasure. Let us/look at the situation and see what important information is/required and how this can be obtained with the minimum/of difficulty.

The reading of a daily newspaper is very/important because it keeps us up to date with current/affairs, and it has a much greater coverage of news/than is presented to us by the television news service./All papers are influential, and most have a political bias./Most people subscribe to a paper with views similar to/their own; one or two papers claim to be altogether/independent and because of this they have an enthusiastic following./

It is important therefore to get into this daily habit/of newspaper reading just as soon as possible. Apart from/this reading, everyone in secretarial work should endeavour to keep/themselves well informed. As well as achieving this object, regular/reading will also extend our vocabulary. This is something which/is essential to people who are working with words. The/wider the understanding of the language the easier it is/to use that language. When taking shorthand notes it is/much easier to write outlines for words of which you/know the meaning and words you will be able to/spell when you transcribe that dictation. A wide general reading/ simply means that you are making your daily job easier/to do, and you will become much more efficient as/a result. An efficient worker usually derives considerable pleasure from/ work; we enjoy doing something if we are good at/it.

For those who have not previously had a reading/habit, and who take steps to do something about it,/it is certainly true to say that they will find/both pleasure and satisfaction in their new interest. Novels, biographies/and some commercial literature should be included in the reading/selection. When working in a specialized field it is important/to familiarize oneself with the special terms and phrases used./Many professional organizations have their own publications and this is/an additional source of information not to be ignored.

Only/an irresponsible individual can afford to adopt an altogether indifferent/attitude. Negligence in keeping oneself informed will result in a/less efficient and less contented worker. (416)

Unit D—Correspondence

1. Read through the following two passages, referring to the key if necessary. Note carefully the outlines for towns and countries which may be new to you.

2. Drill any outlines new to you. Make a fair copy of each letter. Repeat the reading of each letter, noting the time.

Time . . . . . . mins . . . . . . secs

3. Finally, repeat the reading. Aim to read *at least* 30 to 40 words a minute faster than your writing speed, which means that everyone should be reading at a rate of at least 100 words a minute. Note the time taken.

Time . . . . . . mins . . . . . . secs

Letter A

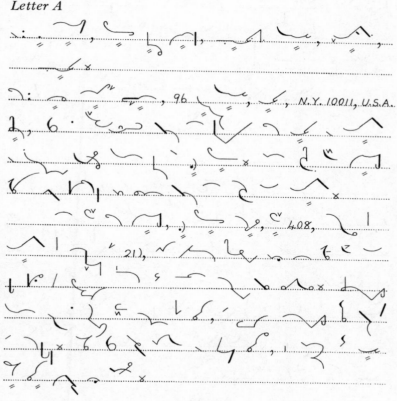

31

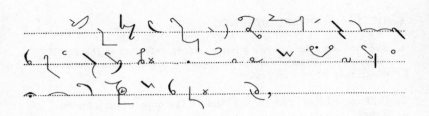

Letter B

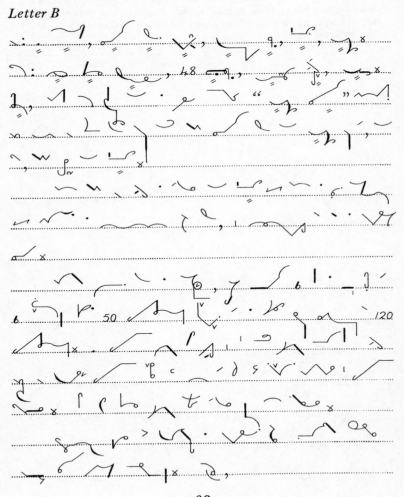

32

Letter A

To: The Manager, African Tours Limited, Kenyatta
      Avenue, Nairobi, Kenya.
From: Miss/Marion Graham, 96 Fifth Avenue, New York,
      N.Y./10011, U.S.A.

Dear Sir,/
    This is a final communication before my departure from
New/York to Nairobi to confirm the various arrangements
for my/tour of East Africa. I am travelling via London and/
this letter should be delivered to you some time before/my
arrival in Nairobi.
    My flight from London, East African/Airways, Flight 408,
arrives at Nairobi at midnight/on the 21st, and I will require
transport to/meet me and thus avoid any difficult delays
which frequently/occur with the commercial airport bus
service. It is important/for me to have an especially quiet
room at the/hotel, and equally important that it is both large
and/air-conditioned. Unless this is possible I will have to/
change hotels, but I am sure that the New Stanley/Hotel will
be able to meet all my requirements.
    I/wish to take advantage of every opportunity to see as/
much as possible of the country and be able to/remember
this trip with both pleasure and satisfaction. The information/
you sent about the safaris you have planned has made/me
very enthusiastic about this tour.
    Yours faithfully,   (218)

Letter B

To: The Manager, Secretarial Staffing Bureau, Victoria
      Street, Auckland, New Zealand./
From: Mr James Stephenson, 48 Grey Street, Newcastle
      upon Tyne,/England.

Dear Sir,
    I read your advertisement in a recent/copy of the "New
Zealand Herald" and I am writing/to you now to ask for
up-to-date information/about secretarial staff in New Zealand
today and, in particular,/about the situation in Auckland.

I am about to open/an office in Auckland—I am a consulting engineer—and/I will need a minimum of three staff, but most/important of all a personal secretary.

I will be looking/for an enthusiastic, intelligent girl who has had a good/training and who has acquired at least 50 words a/minute typewriting and a shorthand speed certificate of 120/words a minute. The work will be largely routine but/ on occasions she will be called upon to travel to/various work sites with me and assist with the compiling/of reports on work progress. At all other times she/will be in charge of the office during my absence./

Please let me have details of the availability of a/person of this calibre as soon as possible together with/the salary range expected.

Yours faithfully,   (206)

Unit E—Technique

Dating the Page

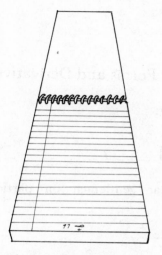

Write the date at the foot of the first
page you use each day.

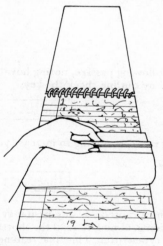

If ever you need to check back on
dictation taken earlier in your notebook
simply flick through the pages until
you reach the required date.

CHAPTER 4

Unit A—Short Forms and Derivatives

Drill the following:

anything   but   dear   gentlemen   on   particular   particularly

satisfactory   this   with

1. Read through the following passage, noting how long it takes you.
   If you cannot read any outline check the key.

   | Time . . . . . . mins . . . . . . secs |

2. Repeat the reading exercise, aiming to increase your reading speed.
   Note your timing.

   | Time . . . . . . mins . . . . . . secs |

3. Drill all outlines which caused you any hesitancy in the last reading.
   Now repeat the reading, aiming to read the shorthand as quickly as
   if the material was typewritten. This final reading should be
   followed by dictation of the passage.

   | Time . . . . . . mins . . . . . . secs |

36

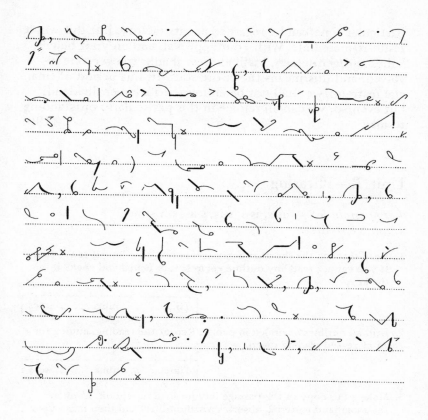

Ladies and gentlemen, I have the satisfaction of present-
ing a/report to you with particularly good results and a much/
larger annual profit. This is somewhat unusual these days,
and/this report is all the more dear to me because/it refutes
all the arguments of the pessimists inside and/outside the
organization. One particular point of satisfaction is the/im-
proved productivity. Anything by way of improvement is
rewarding but/the increased percentage you see in the figures
is remarkable./With the excellent staff we have, this achieve-
ment might not/be considered by some to be particularly
surprising but, ladies/and gentlemen, this staff has had far
larger problems to/face this year than on any other occasion
in the/history of the company. Anything achieved at this

particular time/can be regarded as satisfactory, but this whole result is/incredible. With your approval, and on your behalf, ladies and/gentlemen, I will express thanks to everyone involved, and this/means the entire staff. In this period of financial restraint/we shall not be announcing a larger dividend, but even/so, we can all rejoice in this particularly outstanding result./ (190)

Unit B—Phrasing

Large circle S-S — as-s, is-s, s-is, s-as, s-his/has.
Loop ST — first.

1. Read through the shorthand passage, noting how long it takes you. If you cannot read any outline encircle it in pencil and check it in the key.

Time . . . . . . mins . . . . . . secs

2. Drill all outlines encircled in pencil. Repeat the reading, aiming for an increased reading speed.

Time . . . . . . mins . . . . . . secs

3. Make a fair copy of the passage in your own notebook. Look at the shorthand material, absorb several outlines and then make your own notes without reference to the printed passage. At first you might be able to recall only one complete outline to transfer to your own notes, but with practice you will be able to write several outlines, or a short sentence, without referring to the passage.

4. Now a final reading before receiving the passage from dictation. The aim is to read RAPIDLY.

Time . . . . . . mins . . . . . . secs

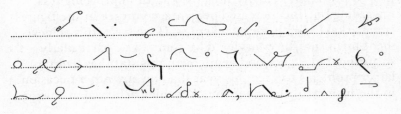

As well as being an excellent qualification when seeking work/shorthand is as useful to the writer in everyday life/as any other personal skill. This subject has so many/uses in a variety of circumstances. First of all, it/will be seen at once how students can take notes/in their other subjects as a result of which studying/is certainly a much easier task. As we have suggested/many times all students should have the opportunity of learning/this subject as soon as possible at school. This has/been discussed over the last few years. It is not/necessary for everyone to be able to write as fast/as the average speed but simply fast enough to make/notes in something more than a brief outline. With such/a skill many students would be able to enjoy lessons/and lectures for the first time. At first people are/not very enthusiastic about this suggestion, but after giving the/matter some consideration there are usually not many against us./Perhaps by Monday next or Friday next you will be/of the same opinion, that is if you are not/so already. The very first step for us to take/as soon as we can is to persuade educational establishments/to act as quickly as possible as we feel enough/time has been wasted.

(224)

Unit C—The Skill of Shorthand Writing

1. The following passage contains information about shorthand writing which should prove to be useful to you as a student shorthand writer. Read through the passage, referring to the key for assistance if necessary.

2. Repeat the reading, noting the time it takes and encircling in pencil any outline which causes hesitancy in reading.

Time . . . . . . mins . . . . . . secs

3. Drill the outlines which caused hesitancy. How many times you drill is a very individual thing. Write the outline several, or many, times repeating it to yourself as you write, until you feel you have it under your control. Now make a final reading of the passage, noting your time, which should show a marked improvement on the first timing, in preparation for receiving the passage from dictation.

Time . . . . . . mins . . . . . . secs

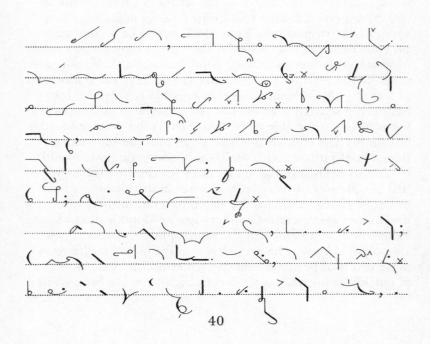

41

As we are well aware, correct posture is very important/in the typewriting room and many demonstrations are given to/emphasize this point. What is not generally appreciated is the/equal necessity for good posture when writing shorthand. At first,/very little attention is given to this, and sometimes none/at all, and yet shorthand writers will never write as/fast as they are capable of doing if they are/not sitting correctly; it is just impossible. Let me enlarge/upon this question; let us have a sensible look and/avoid generalizations.

First of all your feet should be firmly/on the floor, taking the weight of the body; they/should never be crossed or dangling in space, or wrapped/around the chair. It is seen all too easily that/if this is not done the weight distribution of the/body is uneven, the writer tires more quickly and writing/ proficiency is reduced. As soon as possible we should make/ this a matter of routine, and if this has not/been your habit already you will see a remarkable and/satisfactory improvement in your writing stamina.

The non-writing arm/helps to take up the weight of the body by/resting on the desk and at the same time this/ hand is always ready to turn the page. As soon/as you commence writing on the top line of any/page, with forefinger and thumb of the non-writing hand/grasp hold of the bottom corner of the page, but/keep the whole page flat at all times. When the/last line is completed the page is rapidly flicked over/without so much as a fraction of a second being/wasted. Immediately you continue your writing on the first line/of the new page, once again the non-writing arm/takes up the weight of the body, and the finger/and thumb automatically, without you looking, quickly find the corner/of the page, and grasp hold of it. As soon/as this is done you can have a sense of/being in control, knowing that whatever matter is being dictated,/at whatever speed, you will be able to turn the/next page without any problem.

The writing hand throughout all/this page-turning is, of course, writing and it will/be able to do so much more easily, and for/a remarkable period of time, without fatigue, provided, of course,/that the pen is not gripped too tightly. It should/be held just firmly enough to prevent it from falling/out of your hand but never gripped so hard that/ there is a very real danger of it breaking. Try/to keep your fingers straight when writing shorthand irrespective of/how you handle a pen when writing longhand. A tight/ grip and bent fingers make the essential blood supply to/those fingers almost impossible. (474)

Unit D—Correspondence

1. Read through the following two passages, referring to the key if necessary. Note carefully the outlines for towns and countries which may be new to you.

2. Drill any outlines new to you. Make a fair copy of each letter. Repeat the reading of each letter, noting the time.

   | Time . . . . . . mins . . . . . . secs |

3. Finally, repeat the reading. Aim to read *at least* 30 to 40 words a minute faster than your writing speed, which means that everyone should be reading at a rate of at least 100 words a minute. Note the time taken.

   | Time . . . . . . mins . . . . . . secs |

Letter A

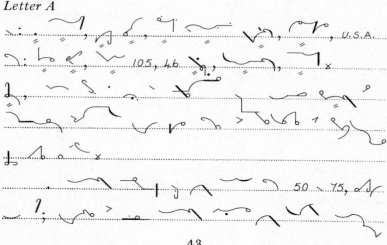

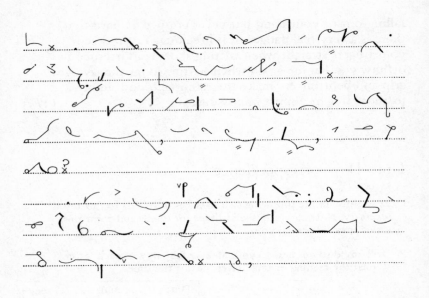

Letter B

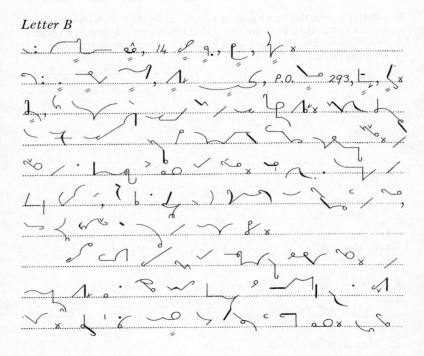

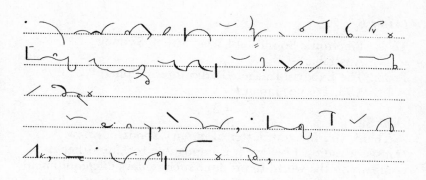

Letter A

To : The Manager, Hilton Hotel, Santa Monica Boulevard, Los Angeles, U./S.A.

From : Thomas Swan, Apartment 105, 46/Bay Street, Vancouver, Canada.

Dear Sir,

I am planning a/meeting of business colleagues to take place next September and/as organizer I would like to have full details from/you of the facilities and the special conference discount rates/you offer.

The number expected to attend will be anything/from 50 to 75, certainly no larger; full particulars/of the exact number and names will be available nearer/the time. The members would be arriving from all parts/of the world and Los Angeles will be a starting/point for these gentlemen for a tour of California and/western Canada.

As well as the details already requested can/you advise me as to the availability of secretarial staff/and interpreters, in particular French and German, and the cost/of such services?

The whole of the financial side will/be handled by me; there is no objection to costs/and although this is something of a generalization I can/be called upon to guarantee any expenses incurred by my/members.

Yours faithfully, (193)

Letter B

To : Electronic Sounds, 14 West Street, Sydney, Australia.

From : The Export Manager,/Radio International, P.O. Box 293, Tokyo, Japan./

Dear Sir,

Thank you for your letter of inquiry about/our new transistor radios. I believe it is impossible for/any other company in the world to produce such remarkable/equipment irrespective of price. Our prices are a demonstration of/the success of our products. All goods leaving the factory/are checked thoroughly and, although it is a generalization to/ say there are never any problems with our products, I/ can assure you that you will find all orders are/entirely satisfactory.

As well as quality we are proud of/our extremely competitive and sensible prices. Our miniature radio is/a masterpiece of modern technology and is guaranteed to have/a wide appeal. It has been on sale in the/United States for the past year with great success. If/you place an order immediately you will be the first/dealer in Australia to handle this line. Documentation and financial/arrangements involved in trading between our two countries are very/ simple.

I am sending you today, by airmail, a demonstration/ model of our latest radio, together with a fully illustrated/ catalogue.

Yours faithfully, (203)

Unit E—Technique

Holding the Pen

Remove pen top and place on the desk. Do not put the pen cap on to the end of the pen because this unbalances the writing instrument.

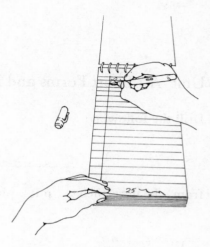

Hold the pen firmly but without great pressure; use a relaxed grip.

Fingers should lie flat along the pen, not arched and squeezing the pen.

Test your pen grip by trying to pull the pen away with your other hand—it should move away easily.

Replace the pen cap after each session of dictation is completed. This will prevent the ink drying out on the nib and the consequent clogging of the ink flow.

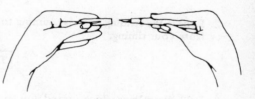

Use two pens with an appreciable difference in the width of the barrel. By changing pens during long dictation sessions the hand pressure is altered, helping towards a more relaxed grip and fighting fatigue.

47

CHAPTER 5

Unit A—Short Forms and Derivatives

Drill the following:

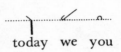

from   I   nevertheless   put   putting   the   to   too/two

today   we   you

1. Read through the following passage, noting how long it takes you.
    If you cannot read any outline check the key.

    > Time . . . . . . mins . . . . . . secs

2. Repeat the reading exercise, aiming to increase your reading speed.
    Note your timing.

    > Time . . . . . . mins . . . . . . secs

3. Drill all outlines which caused you any hesitancy in the last reading.
    Now repeat the reading, aiming to read the shorthand as quickly as
    if the material was typewritten. This final reading should be
    followed by dictation of the passage.

    > Time . . . . . . mins . . . . . . secs

From all I have said today you will have gathered/that
we need to expand the export side of our/business, and by
putting more staff on to this work/I am sure we can be successful. Nevertheless, it is/not quite as simple as that. To attract
extra business,/which will be largely from competitors, we
shall have to/watch both prices and quality. We know we can
put/goods on the market which are equal to any in/quality
but the price has to be attractive. I know/only too well all
the problems we face but, nevertheless,/with your support
I am confident we can succeed. If/the people from the factory can produce the quality goods/for which we are famous
I, in turn, will guarantee/that the sales division will be putting
in all the/extra work needed to find.these additional markets.
The opportunities/today are there and we will take full advantage of/them. You all have an equally important part to play./

From today I shall be putting news of developments on/the staff notice-board and you will be able to/see the progress being made. (195)

Unit B—Phrasing

SHUN — ocean, association.
Intersections (I) T attention — D department — Ch charge — K company, KL Co. Ltd. — F form — N enquiry/inquiry

1. Read through the shorthand passage, noting how long it takes you. If you cannot read any outline encircle it in pencil and check it in the key.

Time . . . . . . mins . . . . . . secs

2. Drill all outlines encircled in pencil. Repeat the reading, aiming for an increased reading speed.

Time . . . . . . mins . . . . . . secs

3. Make a fair copy of the passage in your own notebook. Look at the shorthand material, absorb several outlines and then make your own notes without reference to the printed passage. At first you might be able to recall only one complete outline to transfer to your own notes, but with practice you will be able to write several outlines, or a short sentence, without referring to the passage.

4. Now a final reading before receiving the passage from dictation. The aim is to read RAPIDLY.

Time . . . . . . mins . . . . . . secs

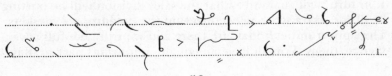

The public will have to make all their enquiries direct/to the head office of this Historical Association. This applies/to any enquiry from both sides of the Atlantic Ocean./This is a worldwide association but most of the work/is done in Britain and the United States. The head/office of this financial company called "The International Historical Trust/Company Limited" is in London. It has one large department/and several smaller departments to handle all of the many/enquiries received each day. Special attention is given to requests/ from students for information about our work. Anyone can join/by completing a simple application form. There is a small/charge to cover the ever-increasing postal costs, but there/is no charge for those under twenty-one years. Your/ attention is called to the work of the Historical Association/ in promoting goodwill between people from all parts of the/ world but in particular to those most involved on either/side of the Atlantic Ocean. This company is a non-profit/making organization and any form of financial support is/always most welcome.

(183)

Unit C—The Skill of Shorthand Writing

1. The following passage contains information about shorthand writing which should prove to be useful to you as a student shorthand writer. Read through the passage, referring to the key for assistance if necessary.

2. Repeat the reading, noting the time it takes and encircling in pencil any outline which causes hesitancy in reading.

Time . . . . . . mins . . . . . . secs

3. Drill the outlines which caused hesitancy. How many times you drill is a very individual thing. Write the outline several, or many, times repeating it to yourself as you write, until you feel you have it under your control. Now make a final reading of the passage, noting your time, which should show a marked improvement on the first timing, in preparation for receiving the passage from dictation.

Time . . . . . . mins . . . . . . secs

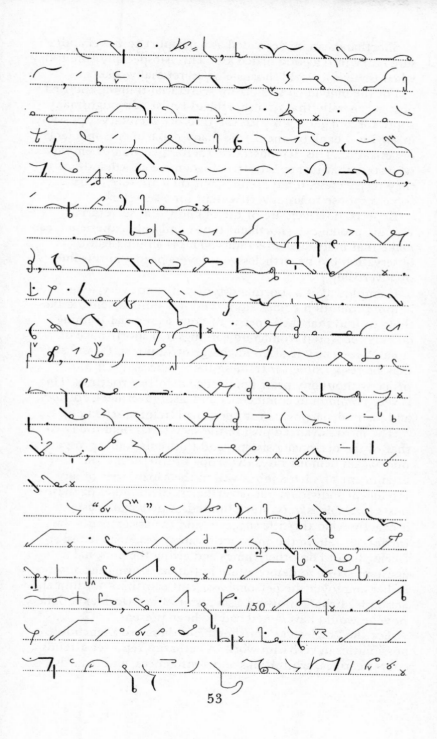

Shorthand can be described as a passport to travel and/a
sure entry into a good office job. This is/especially true today
when there is a world shortage of/secretarial workers.

For the individual fresh from secretarial training the/first
post is generally that of a shorthand-typist, although/many
apply for and get a job with the title/of "secretary", possibly
in the local bank or one of/the many departments in a large
organization. This demonstrates the/desperation of employers
who state that if they advertise for/a mere shorthand-typist
they receive few, if any, replies/but they are sure to have
some response to an/advertisement for a secretary.

Experts, however, are of the opinion/that secretarial
training produces a shorthand-typist and only experience/can
make that individual a secretary. This is an intelligent/
observation but nevertheless employers persist in this line
of advertising./

If employed as a shorthand-typist, it is not very/long
before promotion comes along, and it is quite a/remarkable
thing to find that the expense of your secretarial/training is
quickly recovered from good earnings in a short/space of
time. A secretary is often in charge of/junior staff, and she
may be responsible for training those/who arrive in the
office without any prior knowledge of/office routines. This
is very common in commercial and also/government offices,
and many departments run their own training schemes./

The most advanced post in the secretarial field today is/
that of the personal assistant, and this remarkable progression
once/again demonstrates the scope of this work. The
attainment of/such a job is within the capabilities of any
intelligent/individual but nevertheless the number of these
posts available is/very much limited. A personal assistant
is exactly what the/title suggests, and the assignments she
carries out relieve the/manager of many responsible tasks,
freeing him to do other/things and giving the personal
assistant scope to demonstrate initiative./During the absence
of her employer the personal assistant can/think for him and
act on his behalf knowing, as/a result of her work experience,
how he would have/acted had he been present.

For the "high flyer" in/shorthand there are tremendous
possibilities in verbatim work. A verbatim/reporter attends
court hearings, arbitrations and conferences, and records

the/proceedings, taking down every word spoken. Such work demands absolute/concentration and maximum attention at all times, plus a writing/speed of at least 150 words a/minute. The rewards for such work are as high as/the standards demanded. Trainees for this kind of work are/engaged with lower speeds if they can show potential and/enthusiasm for the challenge which lies ahead. (457)

Unit D—Correspondence

1. Read through the following two passages, referring to the key if necessary. Note carefully the outlines for towns and countries which may be new to you.

2. Drill any outlines new to you. Make a fair copy of each letter. Repeat the reading of each letter, noting the time.

Time . . . . . . mins . . . . . . secs

3. Finally, repeat the reading. Aim to read *at least* 30 to 40 words a minute faster than your writing speed, which means that everyone should be reading at a rate of at least 100 words a minute. Note the time taken.

Time . . . . . . mins . . . . . . secs

Letter A

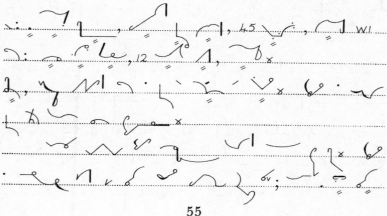

Letter B

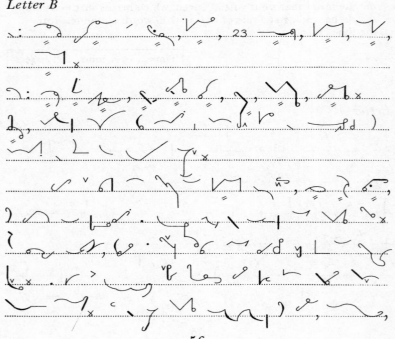

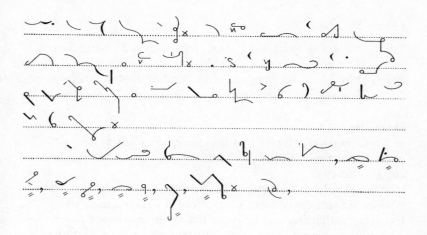

Letter A

To : The Managing Director, World Tours Limited, 45
Piccadilly, London/W1
From: Miss Alice Johnson, 12 North Road, Manchester.

Dear/Sir,

I have just returned from a tour of Rome/and Paris. This
was an individual tour which you arranged/for me some
three weeks ago.

I am sorry to/report that one misadventure followed
another throughout the trip. This/was an expensive holiday
but the hotel standards were not/especially high; in fact the
Grand Hotel in Paris was/positively disappointing. I reserved
a single room with private bathroom/for the duration of my
stay in each city. In/Rome there was only a shower and in
Paris there/was only one bathroom to serve the entire third
floor/on which my bedroom was located.

No attention was paid/to my complaints at either hotel.
As a result of/the generally poor hotel service in Paris I
further complained/to the official tourist office in that city.
The person/in charge promised to look into the matter.

I am/writing to you to make a formal inquiry as to/
whether or not some of my costs are recoverable. An/early
reply is requested.

Yours faithfully,   (196)

Letter B

To: Messrs Wilson and Fraser, Attorneys, 23 King Street, Toronto,/Ontario, Canada.

From : Mrs Janet Richardson, Blue Waters Hotel, Bridgetown, Barbados,/West Indies.

Dear Sirs,

I received your letter this morning/but I am at a loss to understand the contents/so I am writing to ask for further enlightenment.

When/I sold my property in Toronto to your client, Mr/ Arthur Hagan; there were no difficulties concerning the fixtures and/fittings to be included in the purchase price. Although somewhat/unusual, this was a private sale and in the circumstances/I did not take any professional advice. The whole of/the financial side of the transaction was dealt with on/my behalf by my bank manager. With two intelligent parties/involved there was not, in my opinion, any need for/any other form of assistance. Your client's claim that certain/fixtures were removed is quite untrue. The complaint that I/did not mention that a school is to be built/opposite the property is accurate because at the time of/the sale there was no definite information about this proposal./

All further communications on this matter should be addressed to/my attorney, Mr James Ross, Standard House, Main Street, Bridgetown,/Barbados.

Yours faithfully, (203)

Unit E—Technique

Size of Strokes

When reading through your shorthand notes you should never be in any doubt as to whether any stroke is ordinary, half or double length. If the size of strokes is not immediately recognizable it will result in slow and inaccurate transcription.

Be sure, therefore, when writing a double-length or half-length stroke that such strokes are quite distinct and immediately recognizable.

Ordinary

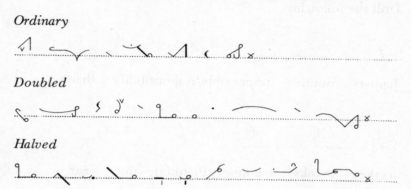

Doubled

Halved

59

Unit A—Short Forms and Derivatives

Drill the following:

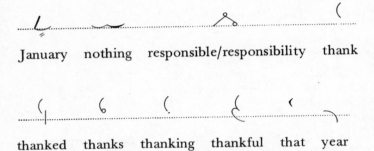

January   nothing   responsible/responsibility   thank

thanked   thanks   thanking   thankful   that   year

1. **Read through the following passage, noting how long it takes you. If you cannot read any outline check the key.**

Time . . . . . . mins . . . . . . secs

2. **Repeat the reading exercise, aiming to increase your reading speed. Note your timing.**

Time . . . . . . mins . . . . . . secs

3. **Drill all outlines which caused you any hesitancy in the last reading. Now repeat the reading, aiming to read the shorthand as quickly as**

if the material was typewritten. This final reading should be
followed by dictation of the passage.

From January this firm will not be held responsible for/
any debts incurred by any employees of the company unless/
there is an agreement to that effect signed in the/current year.
If you have nothing in writing, you should/not extend credit
to any of our employees who may/use your hotel services. It
is thanks to the vigilance/of your accountant that this whole
matter has come to/light and he has been thanked for acting
so promptly./We are thankful that the trouble has been stopped
and/that steps have been taken to prevent it spreading. A/few
years ago it was my responsibility to take similar/action. A

year last January there was a problem when/a credit card had been misused, but really this company/has experienced nothing of a serious nature in this respect./All of our employees who travel on behalf of the/company will have to accept full responsibility for expenditure, and/then claim for the total sum at the end of/each trip. Nothing by way of expenses will be refunded/unless the claims are supported by receipts.(187)

Unit B—Phrasing

R Hook is used in phrasing for shorter forms of:
appear, part, our, far.

1. Read through the shorthand passage, noting how long it takes you. If you cannot read any outline encircle it in pencil and check it in the key.

Time . . . . . . mins . . . . . . secs

2. Drill all outlines encircled in pencil. Repeat the reading, aiming for an increased reading speed.

Time . . . . . . mins . . . . . . secs

3. Make a fair copy of the passage in your own notebook. Look at the shorthand material, absorb several outlines and then make your own notes without reference to the printed passage. At first you might be able to recall only one complete outline to transfer to your own notes, but with practice you will be able to write several outlines, or a short sentence, without referring to the passage.

4. Now a final reading before receiving the passage from dictation. The aim is to read RAPIDLY.

Time . . . . . . mins . . . . . . secs

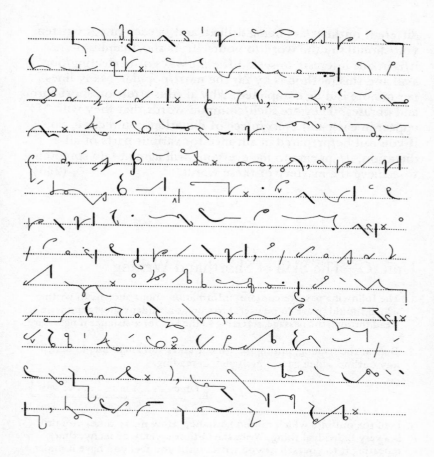

During your training considerable time should be spent on drilling/in order to master certain outlines and to get them/ under strict control. In order that full benefit is gained/from such exercises you should appreciate what you are doing./It is then and only then, I can assure you,/that any progress will be made. Short forms and phrases/for example need drilling in some part of your course,/in fact throughout the course, and usually this is done/in sentence form. Sometimes, however, separate outlines are drilled and/it is most important that this is carried out correctly./A line should be filled with several outlines to be/drilled and then a number of blank lines underneath should/be completed. As each line is completed several different outlines/are being drilled, and as each one is written you/should say the word to yourself. As shorthand writers it/is in our interests to seek different ways of perfecting/our skill and this method is by far the most/popular. Many lines per minute can be completed. Why all/this stress on short forms and phrases? They are such/common words that they will appear in each and every/piece of dictation you receive. So, if you can be/prepared in advance for various parts of all dictation, it/appears to me everyone will agree to do something to/achieve the mastery of these words.   (236)

Unit C—The Skill of Shorthand Writing

1. The following passage contains information about shorthand writing which should prove to be useful to you as a student shorthand writer. Read through the passage, referring to the key for assistance if necessary.

2. Repeat the reading, noting the time it takes and encircling in pencil any outline which causes hesitancy in reading.

> Time . . . . . . mins . . . . . . secs

3. Drill the outlines which caused hesitancy. How many times you drill is a very individual thing. Write the outline several, or many, times repeating it to yourself as you write, until you feel you have it under your control. Now make a final reading of the passage, noting your time, which should show a marked improvement on the first timing, in preparation for receiving the passage from dictation.

> Time . . . . . . mins . . . . . . secs

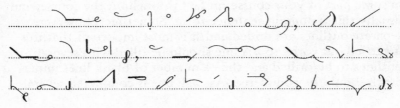

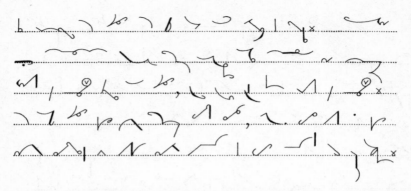

Organization in our training as shorthand writers is essential, whether/we are beginners or advanced students, in order to gain/ the maximum benefit from the time spent. It appears that/ some do not guard against wasting time and do not/accept the responsibility which is clearly their own.

One exercise/which takes little organization is the reading of shorthand. Printed/shorthand from textbooks and magazines should be read with the/aim of reading outlines as quickly as if the page/was typewritten. It is a characteristic of many shorthand writers/that they are poor readers of shorthand, and I can/assure you that the best step to take to improve/your general shorthand skill is to read as much as/you can, and as fast as you can. Push the/speed of your reading as far as possible, and remember/what we are told by the experts and that is,/"The faster you read shorthand the faster you will be/able to write it." There is nothing peculiar about this/ statement, and no one finds the exercise objectionable once she/has started. Follow these instructions and you will find that/there is a marked improvement in your skill within a/ very short space of time. Each year new students find/this identical advice presented to them and, like yourselves, they/ are at liberty to do something about it or to/do nothing.

Read through any piece of shorthand and encircle/the outlines which caused hesitation. After checking from the key,/or seeking help from the teacher, drill those outlines before/reading through the passage once again. On the second reading/your aim should be to read the whole passage without/any hesitation and at a much faster speed than before./

It is in our interests as skill builders to practise/regularly; an irregular and casual approach is useless. If it/is your wish to succeed, and it appears that this/is the case, a routine such as described here will/be immensely helpful.

Some fascinating shorthand reading can be found/in all parts of the monthly magazine "2000". Most/students have it sent to their home and then take/it along to their shorthand class. All the material is/meaningful and you will find that you will want to/read it whether it is to improve your shorthand or/just for the information and pleasure it provides. In order/ that you should gain maximum benefit from your investment in/this magazine you should make sure that you read each/exercise which appears in shorthand, even if you do not/have time to write each exercise. Your knowledge of shorthand/outlines will be very much wider as a result, and/ having once read an outline you will be surprised how/ readily you are able to recall it when called upon/to do so for the first time.   (477)

Unit D—Correspondence

1. Read through the following two passages, referring to the key if necessary. Note carefully the outlines for towns and countries which may be new to you.

2. Drill any outlines new to you. Make a fair copy of each letter. Repeat the reading of each letter, noting the time.

Time . . . . . . mins . . . . . . secs

3. Finally, repeat the reading. Aim to read *at least* 30 to 40 words a minute faster than your writing speed, which means that everyone should be reading at a rate of at least 100 words a minute. Note the time taken.

Time . . . . . . mins . . . . . . secs

67

Letter A

Letter B

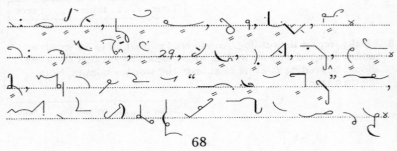

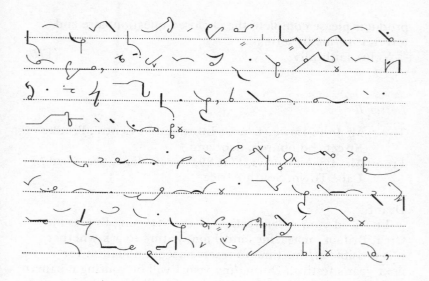

Letter A

To: The President, Caribbean Photographic Supplies
Company, Victoria Street, Kingston, Jamaica./
From: The Director, Omega Optical Company, Berlin,
West Germany.

Dear Sir,/
  It appears from a recent survey made by my trade/
organization that few German products are on sale in the/
Caribbean area. I am writing to distributors throughout
your area/in order that they be made aware of our organization./
  As well as our own fine products this company also/
represents several other manufacturers in northern and
southern Germany. It/has been in our interests to amalgamate
the export side/of our businesses.
  Our products are exported to all parts/of the world but in
particular to England and the/United States of America. I
can assure you that so/far as quality is concerned there are
no finer goods/in the world than those carrying our various
trade marks./
  In order to extend our markets new agencies are being/
established in many countries. If you are interested in our/

products please complete the enclosed questionnaire and
return it to/me by airmail.

    Yours faithfully,   (175)

Letter B

To: Mr John Lowe, Tourist Information Centre, Princes
        Street, Edinburgh, Scotland./
From: Mrs Ivy Matthews, Flat 29, Ocean View, Sea Road,/
        Cape Town, South Africa.

Dear Sir,
    I noticed your recent/article in the "Coming Events in
Great Britain" magazine, and/I am writing to ask whether
it is possible at/this time to reserve accommodation for
next year's festival. During/my visit I will be touring northern
and southern Scotland/but Edinburgh will be my base for
some three weeks,/and that is why I am anxious to have a/
positive reservation. I am told that there is an acute/shortage
of accommodation during the festival, which is becoming
something/of a characteristic of all famous cities.
    If you would/send me a list of hotels and private houses
in/all parts of the city centre I will commence making/
inquiries immediately. A copy of the festival programme
would be/appreciated together with any general information
for a visitor to/Scotland, illustrated brochures and maps.
    Your organization is to be/congratulated on the fine
work it is doing.

    Yours faithfully,/   (180)

Unit E—Technique

Punctuation

Always insert punctuation signs, no matter how obvious you think they will be when you come to transcribe your notes. Punctuation signs are a positive aid to rapid and accurate transcription.

FULL STOP in *one* stroke   either $\times$ or $\propto$

PARENTHESIS (Brackets) $\{$ $\}$

PARAGRAPH   either $/\!/$ or $[$

EXCLAMATION $\mid$ over $\times$

QUESTION $?$ over $\times$

DASH   ⟋

COLON, SEMI-COLON AND COMMA
as in longhand   : ; ,

71

CHAPTER 7

Unit A—Short Forms and Derivatives

Drill the following:

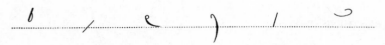

largest   our/hour   several   therefore   which   information

your   yourself   enlarge   Mrs

1. Read through the following passage, noting how long it takes you.
   If you cannot read any outline check the key.

   Time . . . . . . mins . . . . . . secs

2. Repeat the reading exercise, aiming to increase your reading speed.
   Note your timing.

   Time . . . . . . mins . . . . . . secs

3. Drill all outlines which caused you any hesitancy in the last reading.
   Now repeat the reading, aiming to read the shorthand as quickly as
   if the material was typewritten. This final reading should be
   followed by dictation of the passage.

   Time . . . . . . mins . . . . . . secs

We are the largest company in the country and therefore/
we can offer your organization special rates on all your/orders.
Let me enlarge on that statement. Our production costs/are
lower than those of any of our competitors and/this benefit
is passed on to people like yourself. Several/firms have tried
to undercut us, which is only natural/in free enterprise, but
no one has succeeded. Information about/the special offers
which are made several times each year/will be sent to you
on request. It is our/intention to enlarge the range of goods
as soon as/our new showroom opens in January. We shall extend the/hours of opening to include at least one evening so/
that you may visit the premises yourself. Any information
about/credit facilities can be given to you, or your accountant,/
by one of our representatives who will be pleased to/call upon

you at any time. Please, therefore, do not/hesitate to make
an appointment to see a representative and/allow him to give
you full information about the largest/company in the country.

(184)

Unit B—Phrasing

N Hook — been, than, own, not, once.

1. Read through the shorthand passage, noting how long it takes you.
   If you cannot read any outline encircle it in pencil and check it in
   the key.

Time . . . . . . mins . . . . . . secs

2. Drill all outlines encircled in pencil. Repeat the reading, aiming for
   an increased reading speed.

Time . . . . . . mins . . . . . . secs

3. Make a fair copy of the passage in your own notebook. Look at the
   shorthand material, absorb several outlines and then make your own
   notes without reference to the printed passage. At first you might be
   able to recall only one complete outline to transfer to your own
   notes, but with practice you will be able to write several outlines,
   or a short sentence, without referring to the passage.

4. Now a final reading before receiving the passage from dictation. The
   aim is to read RAPIDLY.

Time . . . . . . mins . . . . . . secs

Punctuation is just as important in our shorthand notes as/any outline, and yet this point has been given only/little attention. I have been convinced for more than a/little time that many poor transcriptions are a result of/an almost complete lack of punctuation. When listening to dictation/ some punctuation is so obvious that you believe you will/be able to transcribe without those full stops and commas,/and therefore you do not put them in. Having been/a shorthand writer for longer than you, I say that/as soon as you "hear" punctuation place it in your/notes at once. Punctuated notes are more quickly transcribed than/those without such help when you are typing back; there/is enough work to do in transcription without adding to/it. If you do not already punctuate do not carry/on like this because you are not working at capacity,/you are not helping yourself, and later on I think/you will regret it. (164)

Unit C—The Skill of Shorthand Writing

1. The following passage contains information about shorthand writing which should prove to be useful to you as a student shorthand writer. Read through the passage, referring to the key for assistance if necessary.

2. Repeat the reading, noting the time it takes and encircling in pencil any outline which causes hesitancy in reading.

> Time . . . . . . mins . . . . . . secs

3. Drill the outlines which caused hesitancy. How many times you drill is a very individual thing. Write the outline several, or many, times repeating it to yourself as you write, until you feel you have it under your control. Now make a final reading of the passage, noting your time, which should show a marked improvement on the first timing, in preparation for receiving the passage from dictation.

> Time . . . . . . mins . . . . . . secs

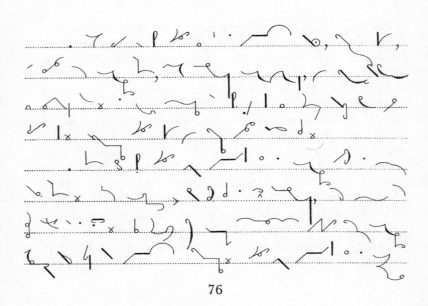

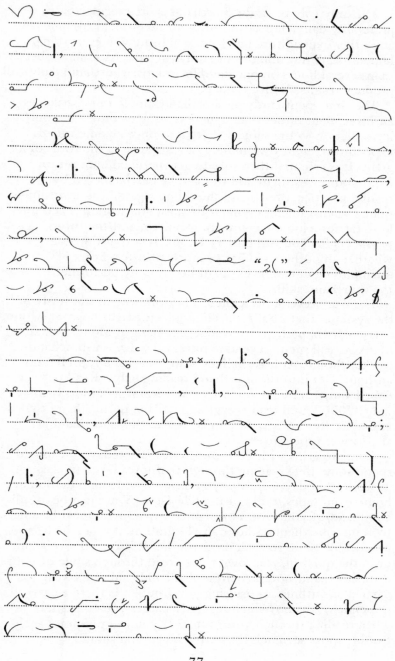

The only way to study shorthand is on a regular/basis, preferably daily, and as a result your investment of/time, and any other expenditure involved, will bring you everything/you hoped for. A few minutes of study each day/is so much better than several hours on one day./To practise shorthand daily will produce results almost at once./

The time spent studying shorthand should be regarded as an/investment rather than a mere passing of time. On your/ introduction to the subject there is at once an amount/of expenditure, your own money or assistance in the form/of a grant. It is essential therefore to get the/maximum return from your investment and this can be best/achieved by regular practice. Shorthand should be regarded as an/insurance policy against unemployment because you will not need to/ look far for a job once you are qualified, and/the future prospects for you will be very bright. It/is questionable whether any other skill has so much to/offer. Fears of unemployment can be extinguished for any performer/of the shorthand skill.

There are several principles to be/followed in the study of the system. First of all/you should decide right now, or within a day or/two, perhaps by Wednesday next or Monday next, that you/will spend several minutes each day on shorthand work at/home. At least half an hour is necessary, preferably an/hour. Get into the shorthand reading habit. Read perfect shorthand/from your textbooks and from the monthly magazine "2000",/and read everything written in shorthand that is available. Remember/the aim is to read that shorthand just as if/it was typewritten.

Come to grips with your own notes./Each day you should spend some time reading through the/notes taken in class, or at work, that day, or/notes you have taken from dictation at home from tapes,/radio or the television. You must be in full command/of your own notes; once written you must be able/ to transcribe them without any hesitation. As soon as it/is practicable to do so each day, whether it is/on a bus or train, or in the quiet of/your own room, read through some of your own shorthand/notes. Analyse them and find out which particular outlines are/causing you trouble. Is there a particular principle of theory/which regularly causes you to hesitate when reading through your/notes? If you can pin-point such trouble spots so/much the better. Then you should immediately revise any weak/theory and drill everything causing any problem. Drill until they/will never again cause you any trouble.

(447)

Unit D—Correspondence

1. Read through the following two passages, referring to the key if necessary. Note carefully the outlines for towns and countries which may be new to you.

2. Drill any outlines new to you. Make a fair copy of each letter. Repeat the reading of each letter, noting the time.

Time . . . . . . mins . . . . . . secs

3. Finally, repeat the reading. Aim to read *at least* 30 to 40 words a minute faster than your writing speed, which means that everyone should be reading at a rate of at least 100 words a minute. Note the time taken.

Time . . . . . . mins . . . . . . secs

Letter A

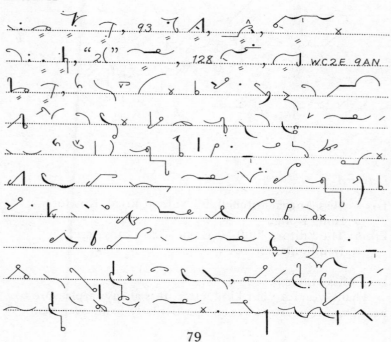

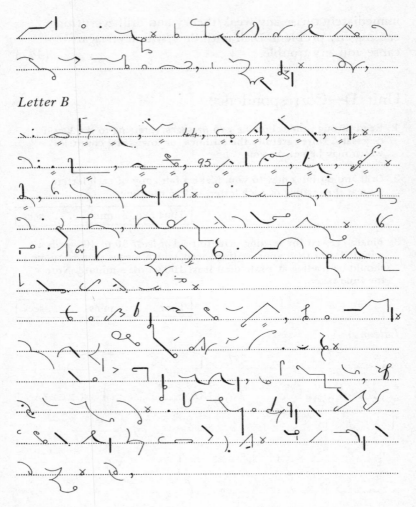

Letter B

Letter A

To : Miss Angela Mitchell, 93 Nathan Road, Kowloon,
      Hong Kong./
From: The Editor, 2000 Magazine, 128 Long Acre,
      London/WC2E 9AN

Dear Miss Mitchell,/
    Thank you for your kind letter. It is always a/pleasure to
hear from regular readers and particularly from overseas./

It was most interesting to have your views on the/magazine and to know that you find it so instructive/and that it has had such a good influence on/your own shorthand skill. We do everything we can to/make the magazine appealing as well as instructive and therefore/it is always a delight to all of us within/the organization to receive letters such as yours.

As we/have the largest circulation of any magazine of this kind/I am sure you will have a good response to/your proposed advertisement. More than ever before, secretaries are travelling/ throughout the world, and many advertise for posts in the/ magazine. The expenditure involved should be regarded as an investment./It is questionable whether you will receive replies from employers/in all the countries you mention, but I am sure/you will not be disappointed.

Yours sincerely, (197)

Letter B

To : Mr Donald Irving, Apartment 44, Queen's Road, Bombay, India./
From : The Director, Medical Supplies Company, 95 Rue de Lausanne,/Geneva, Switzerland.

Dear Sir,

Thank you for your order received/yesterday. As a new customer, without any introduction from an/established customer, it will be necessary to take up your/banker's reference. This will cause a slight delay but I/am sure you will appreciate that this is a regular/procedure we have to take at the beginning when opening/new accounts.

This company is one of the largest distributors/of medical supplies in Europe, and satisfaction is guaranteed. Your/order will be shipped as soon as possible and certainly/not later than the end of this month.

Because of/the great distance involved, if it is at all practicable/for you, I would suggest air freight for any future/ orders. The additional expenditure is generally considered to be worth/while with supplies being received so much quicker than by/the sea route. All goods are covered by your own/insurance.

Yours faithfully, (173)

Unit E—Technique

Posture

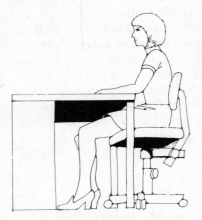

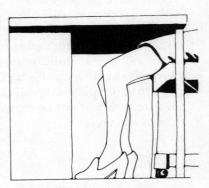

Both feet flat on the floor; back supported by the chair.

One foot slightly in front of the other.

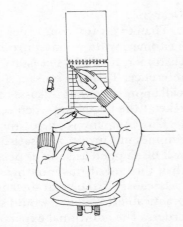

Weight of the body on the non-writing arm, and the hand of that arm holding the corner of the notebook page ready to turn.

Notebook at right-angles to the desk. Start writing on the first line and complete the page line by line with the page completely flat—it is only moved when turning to the next page.

CHAPTER 8

Unit A—Short Forms and Derivatives

Drill the following:

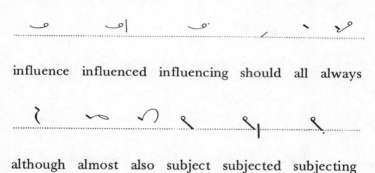

influence influenced influencing should all always

although almost also subject subjected subjecting

1. Read through the following passage, noting how long it takes you.
   If you cannot read any outline check the key.

   | Time . . . . . . mins . . . . . . secs |

2. Repeat the reading exercise, aiming to increase your reading speed.
   Note your timing.

   | Time . . . . . . mins . . . . . . secs |

3. Drill all outlines which caused you any hesitancy in the last reading. Now repeat the reading, aiming to read the shorthand as quickly as if the material was typewritten. This final reading should be followed by dictation of the passage.

Time . . . . . . mins . . . . . . secs

It is always interesting to think about what particularly influenced/us to take up the study of shorthand. Although almost/everyone will consider that it was an obvious choice of/subject for anyone wanting to work in the secretarial field,/ there will always be someone else who will say that/the biggest influencing factor was something quite different. Perhaps it/was the simple fascination of watching a person writing

84

shorthand/years before which was the main influence in beginning a/course of study. There should always be a certain
amount/of fascination about any skill subject in which we
decide/to invest time. There should also be an element of/
determination to succeed. So many things influence our
lives all/the time, and we in turn are subjecting friends and/
colleagues to our way of thinking. Although all of us/are
largely unaware of the many influencing powers around us,/
it is always worth looking back and considering just what/it
was that influenced us to take a particular subject/at school
or college. (174)

Unit B—Phrasing

F/V Hook — have, of, off, event.

1. Read through the shorthand passage, noting how long it takes you.
   If you cannot read any outline encircle it in pencil and check it in
   the key.

   Time . . . . . . mins . . . . . . secs

2. Drill all outlines encircled in pencil. Repeat the reading, aiming for
   an increased reading speed.

   Time . . . . . . mins . . . . . . secs

3. Make a fair copy of the passage in your own notebook. Look at the
   shorthand material, absorb several outlines and then make your own
   notes without reference to the printed passage. At first you might be
   able to recall only one complete outline to transfer to your own
   notes, but with practice you will be able to write several outlines,
   or a short sentence, without referring to the passage.

4. Now a final reading before receiving the passage from dictation. The
   aim is to read RAPIDLY.

   Time . . . . . . mins . . . . . . secs

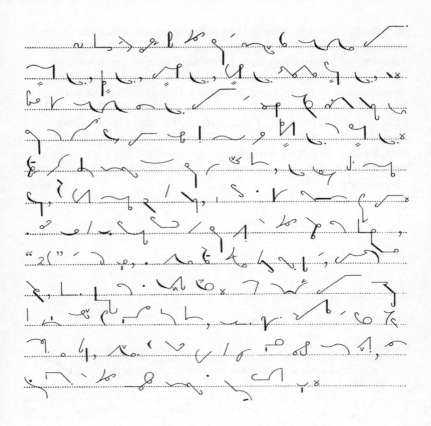

You have taken up the serious study of shorthand speed/and you may find this involves working Monday evening, Tuesday/evening, Wednesday evening, Thursday evening and perhaps Friday evening, too./At all events it will involve some evening work and/to succeed in this subject you will be better off/if you spread your learning over the week instead of/doing many hours on Saturday evening or Sunday evening. Those/who have the real desire to improve in their speed/will find the time, even if it is only ten/minutes every day, although thirty minutes would be much better,/but plan a daily programme throughout the week. The sort/of things which need plenty of application are speed reading/of shorthand passages from textbooks, "2000" and your/own notes, the review of those short forms which have/been proving difficult and, whenever possible, taking dictation from a/variety of voices. Much remedial work can be done at/home in spite of other calls on your time, including/drilling of words and phrases until complete mastery is achieved,/revising that part of theory which still causes hesitation in/your writing, and some fair copying of shorthand exercises to/improve a poor quality note.

(205)

Unit C—The Skill of Shorthand Writing

1. The following passage contains information about shorthand writing which should prove to be useful to you as a student shorthand writer. Read through the passage, referring to the key for assistance if necessary.

2. Repeat the reading, noting the time it takes and encircling in pencil any outline which causes hesitancy in reading.

Time . . . . . . mins . . . . . . secs

3. Drill the outlines which caused hesitancy. How many times you drill is a very individual thing. Write the outline several, or many, times repeating it to yourself as you write, until you feel you have it under your control. Now make a final reading of the passage, noting your time, which should show a marked improvement on the first timing, in preparation for receiving the passage from dictation.

Time . . . . . . mins . . . . . . secs

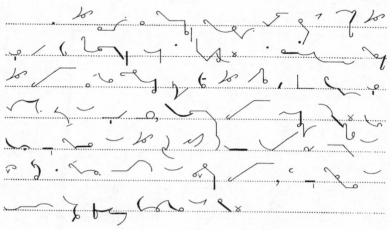

88

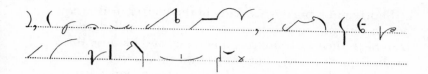

The shorthand skill is practised principally to record speech and/the majority of shorthand notes are then transcribed into a/typewritten form. A significant percentage of shorthand work is office/correspondence but there are those shorthand writers who take verbatim/notes of lengthy hearings in court cases, bankruptcy work and/industrial arbitrations. If you have made good progress in shorthand/so far and wish to go further you should keep/in mind that there is a promising career in high-/speed work, with good prospects in income for those who/distinguish themselves in the subject.

Why is high speed necessary?/During an exchange of questions and answers in any hearing/you can expect some rapid speech, and whilst the administrator/in charge of the investigation does keep control, human feelings/do at times get out of hand. During cross-examination,/for example, there might well be a heated exchange between/the principal parties involved. It is at times such as/these that the high-speed reserve comes into play, and/the shorthand writer who has sufficient speed can easily get/out of what otherwise might be a difficult few minutes./

For just this same reason it is important for you/to have a speed reserve when entering any shorthand examination./A substantial number of candidates fail a speed test because/ they entered for a speed which they could only just/take down and for which they had no extra reserve./To be successful at any given speed you should be/able to write at 20 words a minute above that/speed for at least one minute.

All dictation contains a/high proportion of easy words but you have to have/that speed reserve when you meet that inconvenient, new or/unusual word, or when you encounter a sudden increase in/speed. Because of the frequency in all speech of certain/words it is important for shorthand writers to master such/outlines. A good preliminary step towards speed building is to/check through the 700 common words list and make/sure that none of them is a stranger to you;/ make sure that each one is completely at your command./

Shorthand reporters working in the courts, arbitrations and in various/organizations, are frequently called upon to read back their notes/during a hearing, and because this might happen at any/time they write good accurate shorthand which can be read/without hesitation. First of all they mastered those common words/and gradually built up their shorthand vocabulary. Even so, they/still meet new words regularly, and whenever they do those/outlines are later drilled and brought under total command.   (439)

Unit D—Correspondence

1. Read through the following two passages, referring to the key if necessary. Note carefully the outlines for towns and countries which may be new to you.

2. Drill any outlines new to you. Make a fair copy of each letter. Repeat the reading of each letter, noting the time.

> Time . . . . . . mins . . . . . . secs

3. Finally, repeat the reading. Aim to read *at least* 30 to 40 words a minute faster than your writing speed, which means that everyone should be reading at a rate of at least 100 words a minute. Note the time taken.

> Time . . . . . . mins . . . . . . secs

Letter A

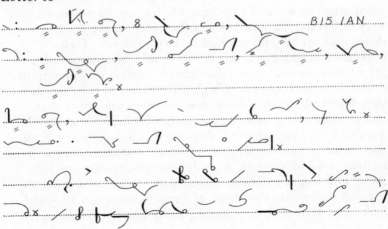

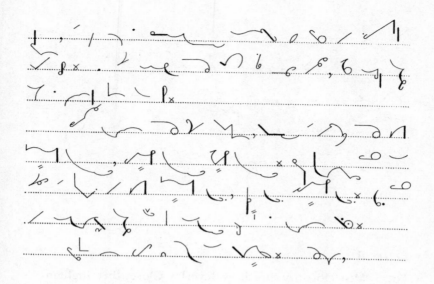

Letter B

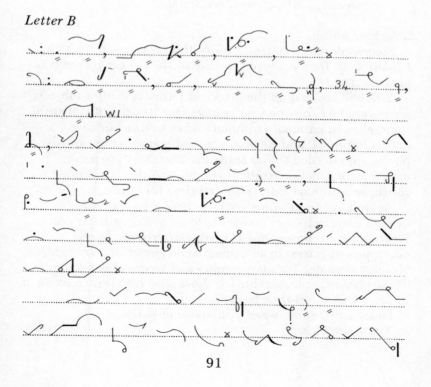

91

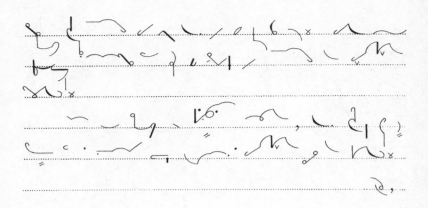

Letter A

To: Miss Dorothy Smith, 8 Beverley Close, Birmingham
B15/1AN
From: The Principal, Northern Secretarial College, Royal
Avenue,/Belfast, Northern Ireland.

Dear Miss Smith,
    I received your letter/of inquiry this morning, for which
I thank you. I/am enclosing a copy of the college prospectus
as requested./
    You will see that all the principal business studies subjects/
are covered by the one-year course. Our students distinguish/
themselves in national examinations as well as our own
college/diploma, and each year a significant number of first
places/are awarded to our students. The short intensive
course also/achieves excellent results, and this is intended
for those who/have only a limited time for study.
    As well as/the full-time courses there are part-time,
beginner and/refresher courses held on Monday afternoon,
Wednesday afternoon and Thursday/afternoon. Speed
development classes in shorthand and typewriting are held/on
Monday evening, Tuesday evening and Wednesday evening.
These classes/are invaluable for those who find it inconvenient
to attend/on a full-time basis.
    Please contact me when you/arrive in Belfast.
    Yours sincerely,   (185)

Letter B

To: The Manager, Kilimanjaro Hotel, Dar es Salaam, Tanzania.

From: Mr John/Crosby, Secretary, Wild Life Protection Society, 34 Oxford Street,/London W1

Dear Sir,

I wish to reserve a/single room with private bath for the month of April./I will be on a tour of inspection of game/ reserves in East Africa, and during my extended stay in/ Tanzania I will make Dar es Salaam my base. The/principal aim of my tour is to inspect conditions within/the various game reserves and to report back to my/headquarters.

Many of our members are interested in visiting East/Africa and we expect to run regular tours in the/near future. If we have sufficient response to our proposed/substantial advertising campaign we should be having our first tour/this year. We have many distinguished members in our society/ who have supported our campaign for wild life preservation.

I/am no stranger to Dar es Salaam myself, having travelled/ throughout East Africa with a camera crew filming a wild/life series for television.

Yours faithfully, (176)

Unit E—Technique

How to Use the Notebook

Keep the book open flat on the desk.
Do not fold pages underneath each
other.

Rule a left-side margin (with
sufficient pages ruled to last a
dictation session) and use as
instructed in Chapter 2.

Each day, date the page as instructed
in Chapter 3.

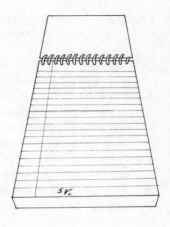

After completing the transcription
of each page of notes place a large
tick or diagonal line across the page.

If the notebook has a firm cover use
an elastic band around the cover.
When pages have been transcribed
fold them under the band. When
taking dictation your notebook will
then open at a clean page.

Write across the full width of each
page, except for the margin, aiming
to write 12-14 outlines per line.
(Halving the page down the centre
and completing each half is of little
value in general work; this technique
is only good for Question and Answer
routines.)

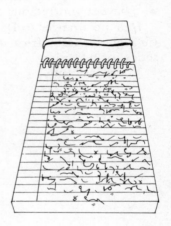

CHAPTER 9

Unit A—Short Forms and Derivatives

Drill the following:

gentleman   there/their   think   thinking   enlargement

before   cannot   difficulty   immediate   immediately

1. Read through the following passage, noting how long it takes you. If you cannot read any outline check the key.

   Time . . . . . . mins . . . . . . secs

2. Repeat the reading exercise, aiming to increase your reading speed. Note your timing.

   Time . . . . . . mins . . . . . . secs

3. Drill all outlines which caused you any hesitancy in the last reading. Now repeat the reading, aiming to read the shorthand as quickly as if the material was typewritten. This final reading should be followed by dictation of the passage.

   Time . . . . . . mins . . . . . . secs

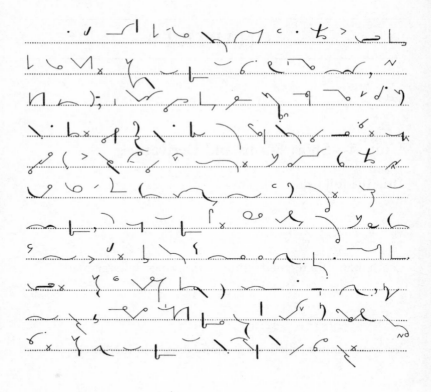

A gentleman called at the office before lunch with an/
enlargement of the photograph taken at the office party. I/
think there will be no difficulty in selling several copies/im-
mediately, and I told him so, but apparently he cannot/take
the risk of producing extra copies on the chance/of there
being a demand. He said there would have/to be a definite
order placed before he goes ahead./No doubt he was thinking
of the possible loss he/might incur. I shall circulate this enlargement round the various/offices and ask them to let me
have the money/with their orders. I cannot see any immediate
difficulty, or/indeed any difficulty at all. As soon as I receive/
the orders I shall send them with the money to/the gentleman.
It would appear that he makes his living/touring the country

taking photographs. I think that with his/personality it must be easy to make a good living,/but there are many people who would experience untold difficulties/if they had to rely on their persuasive powers of/selling. I think he should have no difficulty in being/employed by our sales people.   (195)

Unit B—Phrasing

L Hook — all, only.

1. Read through the shorthand passage, noting how long it takes you. If you cannot read any outline encircle it in pencil and check it in the key.

> Time . . . . . . mins . . . . . . secs

2. Drill all outlines encircled in pencil. Repeat the reading, aiming for an increased reading speed.

> Time . . . . . . mins . . . . . . secs

3. Make a fair copy of the passage in your own notebook. Look at the shorthand material, absorb several outlines and then make your own notes without reference to the printed passage. At first you might be able to recall only one complete outline to transfer to your own notes, but with practice you will be able to write several outlines, or a short sentence, without referring to the passage.

4. Now a final reading before receiving the passage from dictation. The aim is to read RAPIDLY.

> Time . . . . . . mins . . . . . . secs

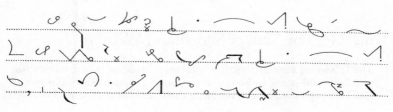

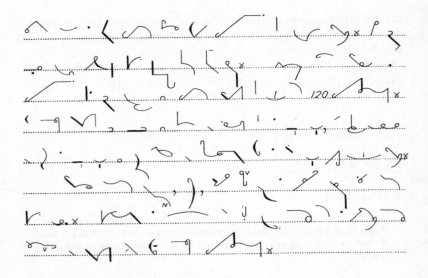

What is speed in shorthand? It is only a matter/of writing faster and faster and many ask what is/the purpose of that. I suppose everyone will agree that/it is only a matter of writing faster, but to/have also a reserve ready at all times is invaluable./No employees can be happy in a job where at/all times they are working at full pressure. Such would/be the case if you received daily dictation at your/top speed. How much more pleasant the working day would/be if only you were able to write at one/hundred or one hundred and twenty words a minute. That/extra ability would give you time to concentrate on a/good note, and it is only common sense to say/that a good note is easier and faster to transcribe/than a bad note written under pressure.

By all means/in your power, therefore, always strive to have a reserve/of speed ahead of your daily needs. It will only/be a matter of attending evening courses or a refresher/ course of some kind to build up those extra words/a minute.

(192)

Unit C—The Skill of Shorthand Writing

1. The following passage contains information about shorthand writing which should prove to be useful to you as a student shorthand writer. Read through the passage, referring to the key for assistance if necessary.

2. Repeat the reading, noting the time it takes and encircling in pencil any outline which causes hesitancy in reading.

> Time . . . . . . mins . . . . . . secs

3. Drill the outlines which caused hesitancy. How many times you drill is a very individual thing. Write the outline several, or many, times repeating it to yourself as you write, until you feel you have it under your control. Now make a final reading of the passage, noting your time, which should show a marked improvement on the first timing, in preparation for receiving the passage from dictation.

> Time . . . . . . mins . . . . . . secs

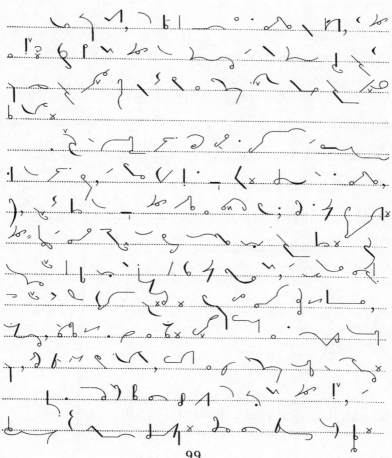

Have you heard already, or does it come as a/surprise to
be told, that shorthand is dying? This has/been said about
shorthand for so many years and by/so many different people

100

that today most people realize the/truth to be that the subject is very much alive/because the public recognizes its value.

The arrival of electrical/recording machines was a welcome and significant aid for recording/speech, and by all accounts they are doing a good/job. It is something of a surprise, therefore, to find/that the demand for good shorthand writers is higher than/ever; there is a shortage throughout the world. Shorthand-typists/and secretaries cannot be found in sufficient numbers to meet/the public demand. Established firms find it difficult to meet/all contingencies which this shortage brings about, and new companies/ simply cannot find all the staff they would like to/have. Everybody wants secretarial assistance — doctors, engineers, solicitors — the list/is endless. Whilst quantity is an important factor today, and/there is just not the supply available, quality is still/of very much interest to employers.

During the course of/their studies some students read or hear about shorthand dying,/and it is only natural that they should become discouraged./There seems some justification for their dissatisfaction. Independent surveys show,/however, that no student should be at all concerned because/there is no significance to be attached to such reports./Certain vested interests with selfish motives seem to be at/work. At regular intervals there is an amalgamation of such/interests incorporated into one general publicity campaign, but identification of/the influence behind the scenes remains a mystery.

The skill/of shorthand has been acquired by millions throughout the world,/and it has served them well. Once learned it is/never forgotten and many people continue to use it as/a personal skill after they no longer require it in/ their daily work. Who learns shorthand? Boys and girls, men/and women from all walks of life and in all/parts of the world. Usually the subject is studied at/school or college from the age of 14 or 15,/and it is found to be an immensely useful skill,/and one which impresses employers. Anyone considering entering office work/will find it invaluable, and for secretarial workers it is/essential. Many people learn the subject after leaving university with/a degree to enable them to get a job; a/degree alone is often not enough. To make it

101

a/really worthwhile qualification you should aim for a
minimum speed/of 100 words a minute, preferably 120/
words a minute. Speeds lower than 100 might/be useful but
as longhand can be written at about/60 words a minute a
shorthand speed of under 100/words a minute is not much
to boast about./ (480)

Unit D—Correspondence

1. Read through the following two passages, referring to the key if
   necessary. Note carefully the outlines for towns and countries
   which may be new to you.

2. Drill any outlines new to you. Make a fair copy of each letter.
   Repeat the reading of each letter, noting the time.

   > Time . . . . . . mins . . . . . . secs

3. Finally, repeat the reading. Aim to read *at least* 30 to 40 words a
   minute faster than your writing speed, which means that everyone
   should be reading at a rate of at least 100 words a minute. Note
   the time taken.

   > Time . . . . . . mins . . . . . . secs

Letter A

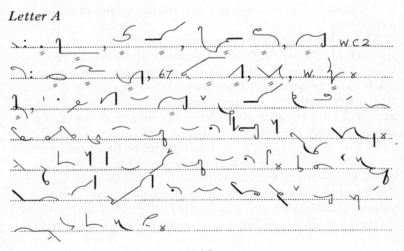

102

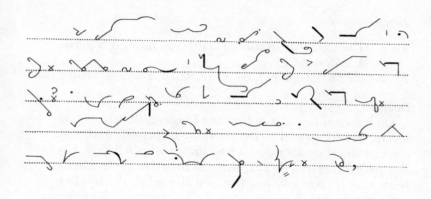

Letter B

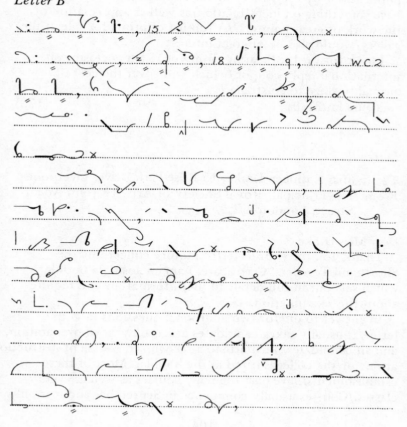

To: The Director, National Gallery, Trafalgar Square,
        London WC2/
From: Mr Michael Field, 67 York Road, Perth, W. Australia./

Dear Sir,
    On a recent holiday in London I visited/the gallery on
several occasions and to my pleasant surprise/found my
interest in art greater than I had previously/believed. Up to
this time I had had no real/interest in art at all. It would
seem that I/have only just become alerted to the world of
art/and now by all means possible I intend to try/and make
up for the time I have lost.
    I/would welcome any information you have concerning
publications by the/gallery on art appreciation. Perhaps you
have something on identification/as well as appreciation of
the work of great painters?/A full list of prints for sale at the
gallery/would also be of great interest.
    I look forward to/hearing from you. I am enclosing an
international reply coupon/which will cover the cost of
airmail postage to Australia./
    Yours faithfully,   (172)

Letter B

To: Miss Kathleen Drake, 15 Rose Park Drive, Liverpool.
From: The Principal,/Royal Society of Arts, 18 John Adam
        Street, London W/C2.

Dear Miss Drake,
    Thank you for your letter/of inquiry concerning the
Shorthand Teachers' Certificate. I am enclosing/a booklet
which sets out in full detail all the/information you require
about this examination.
    In answer to one/or two additional questions in your
letter, it usually takes/candidates at least a year of preparation,
and all candidates/must attend a recognized course of instruction
at one of/the colleges listed in the booklet. Most of these
establishments/have part-time day courses as well as evening
classes./Courses usually commence in September and it is only

a/matter of you contacting your local college and arranging
when/you must attend to enrol.

As you will see, the/Society has a list of recommended
reading, and it is/usual for the lecturers at your local college
to give/further guidance. The examination can be taken in
May and/November.

Yours sincerely,   (173)

Unit E—Technique

Making the Best Use of the Working Area

Keep your desk at school or college clear of articles other than those you will need in the shorthand lesson. Make space to allow your notebook to lie flat on the desk.

All articles surplus to your needs during shorthand should be put away, preferably out of sight and certainly out of the path of colleagues and teacher.

The "tidy desk" routine should go with you into the office. A cluttered desk does suggest a similar mind.

CHAPTER 10

Unit A—Short Forms and Derivatives

Drill the following:

could   eye   in   trade/toward   trades/towards   trader   who

without   is   shall   will

1. Read through the following passage, noting how long it takes you.
    If you cannot read any outline check the key.

Time . . . . . . mins . . . . . . secs

2. Repeat the reading exercise, aiming to increase your reading speed.
    Note your timing.

Time . . . . . . mins . . . . . . secs

3. Drill all outlines which caused you any hesitancy in the last reading.
    Now repeat the reading, aiming to read the shorthand as quickly as
    if the material was typewritten. This final reading should be
    followed by dictation of the passage.

Time . . . . . . mins . . . . . . secs

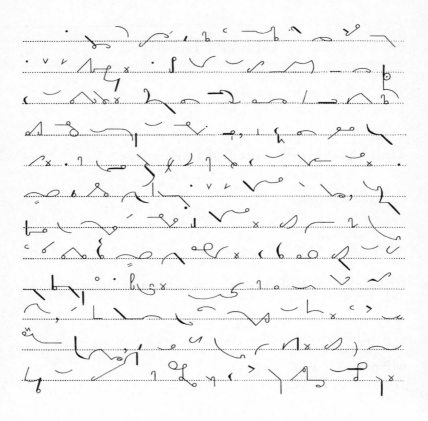

A businessman or woman who trades with countries abroad
must/always keep an eye on the rate of exchange. A/sudden
fall in one currency could mean disaster without any/hope of
compensation. There may be some government schemes which/
give help towards certain expenses incurred in exporting goods,
but/without doubt some risks have to be run. The trade/figures
published each month show the true position without any/
political influence. The Minister who is responsible will have
to/keep an eye on the balance of payments, for there/could
be difficulties if imports and exports do not balance./We shall
look toward the future with high hopes that/this Minister will
be successful. Without this success we shall/be in what could

be described as a state of/confusion. International trade is now part of modern life, and/it could become even more important in time. With all/the new scientific developments, who knows what the future will/hold. We shall see many changes in world trade as/soon as it is.possible to trade without all the/petty restrictions in existence today. (185)

Unit B—Phrasing

Omissions — a word, a repeated consonant, initial R hook, a final hook or a syllable.

1. Read through the shorthand passage, noting how long it takes you. If you cannot read any outline encircle it in pencil and check it in the key.

Time . . . . . . mins . . . . . . secs

2. Drill all outlines encircled in pencil. Repeat the reading, aiming for an increased reading speed.

Time . . . . . . mins . . . . . . secs

3. Make a fair copy of the passage in your own notebook. Look at the shorthand material, absorb several outlines and then make your own notes without reference to the printed passage. At first you might be able to recall only one complete outline to transfer to your own notes, but with practice you will be able to write several outlines, or a short sentence, without referring to the passage.

4. Now a final reading before receiving the passage from dictation. The aim is to read RAPIDLY.

Time . . . . . . mins . . . . . . secs

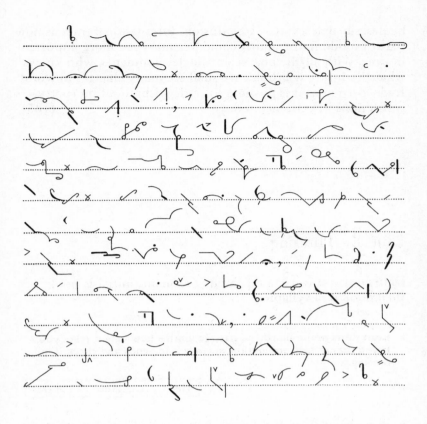

Addressing envelopes correctly enables the Post Office to perform its/function of delivering mail very much faster. Sometimes the Post/Office is faced with an almost impossible task of reading/bad writing, and the delays that follow are costly to/everyone. If we are to have satisfactory results in this/direction and avoid additional heavy expenses we must follow instructions./Many countries now use postal codes and as soon as/possible these should be used by everyone. One or two/people seem to think this is not important but such/people should bear in mind that no system is likely/to be successful if it does not have the full/co-operation of the public. Again and again appeals for such/co-operation are made, and each time there is a larger/and larger response and it simply must be a sign/of the times that these requests have to be repeated/so frequently. If there is no code for an area,/

a first-rate alternative is to type the name of/the town or city in closed capitals which will be/so much easier for the Post Office workers to understand/than it would have been if typed in the same/style as the rest of the address.   (207)

Unit C—The Skill of Shorthand Writing

1. The following passage contains information about shorthand writing which should prove to be useful to you as a student shorthand writer. Read through the passage, referring to the key for assistance if necessary.

2. Repeat the reading, noting the time it takes and encircling in pencil any outline which causes hesitancy in reading.

> Time . . . . . . mins . . . . . . secs

3. Drill the outlines which caused hesitancy. How many times you drill is a very individual thing. Write the outline several, or many, times repeating it to yourself as you write, until you feel you have it under your control. Now make a final reading of the passage, noting your time, which should show a marked improvement on the first timing, in preparation for receiving the passage from dictation.

> Time . . . . . . mins . . . . . . secs

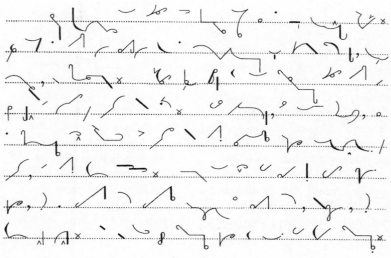

112

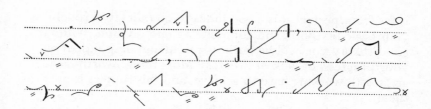

Speed development in shorthand cannot take place unless there is/a good foundation of theory. Without such knowledge a writer/will certainly have an imperfect note which will be very/difficult, if not impossible, to transcribe. On the other hand/it is not suggested that any prospective shorthand writer should/sit down and learn each rule by heart. What is/required, and is in fact essential, is a tremendous amount/of application of the rules by writing hundreds of outlines/involving each rule, and writing them again and again. Keep/in mind what you are doing when drilling outlines, saying/the word or words to yourself as you write or,/better still, saying them out loud. All too often students/practise outlines without knowing what they are practising.

It is/most important to concentrate when practising, and this is just/not possible when one is distracted by some form of/entertainment on the radio or television. Very few can subscribe/to the theory of those who claim that they study/ better in a noisy atmosphere.

Satisfactory results are seldom achieved/without some real effort. Precious time will have to be/given hour by hour during the period of study, and/a definite plan of work should be decided upon to/gain the maximum benefit. All of the theory should be/revised regularly, even after the beginning of speed development, right/up to writing at high speeds. All short forms and/intersections should be "kept on the boil", that is read,/drilled and applied regularly; these outlines have to be mastered/or else they will master you. Get down to some/serious work on them, and once they have become a/part of you make sure they are brought into frequent/use by planned practice.

Once again you should bear in/mind that daily practice is much better than one or/two hours at the weekend. If you want to develop/your speed but know that your theory is far from/perfect it is a good idea to go quickly through/ your basic textbook and complete a rapid revision. Without good/theory you will be both surprised and despondent at your/progress, or lack of progress. Most things worth having are/worth working hard to achieve, and this subject is one/of them.

If you find yourself repeatedly making errors involving/one particular part of theory you should then make a/real effort to come to grips with that section, drilling/the examples given in the textbook and possibly referring to/a different text for a new presentation of the rule/and additional examples.

The shorthand system you are writing is/used throughout the world, from New York in the United/States to Nairobi in Kenya, from London in England to/Wellington in New Zealand. Millions of people write Pitman's Shorthand./It is certainly a worthwhile qualification. (476)

Unit D—Correspondence

1. Read through the following two passages, referring to the key if necessary. Note carefully the outlines for towns and countries which may be new to you.

2. Drill any outlines new to you. Make a fair copy of each letter. Repeat the reading of each letter, noting the time.

   Time . . . . . . mins . . . . . . secs

3. Finally, repeat the reading. Aim to read *at least* 30 to 40 words a minute faster than your writing speed, which means that everyone should be reading at a rate of at least 100 words a minute. Note the time taken.

   Time . . . . . . mins . . . . . . secs

Letter A

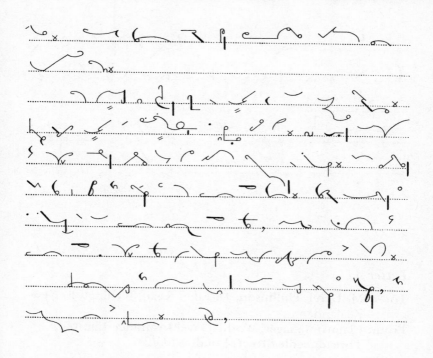

Letter B

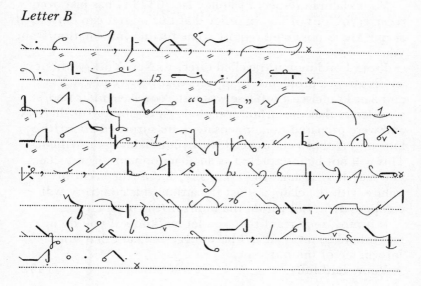

115

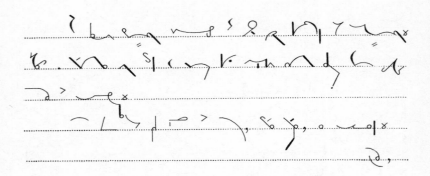

Letter A

To: Mr Derek Phillipson, 18 Eden Road, Wellington, New
Zealand.
From: Claims/Manager, World Travel Insurance Limited,
Threadneedle Street, London EC/2

Dear Sir,
    Your claim in respect of Policy No./637384 has just been
received/by this office. In order that this matter can be/settled
as quickly as possible I require some further information/from
you.
    From London you travelled direct to New York/without
any insurance problems. It appears that between New York/
and San Francisco a suitcase was lost. You have indicated/in
your letter that the airline accepted responsibility for the/loss
and were prepared to compensate. I am surprised about/this
but suggest that you proceed with your claim against/them.
This will not be interpreted as an abandonment of/any claim
you may have against this company, and in/the event of
failure with the claim against the airline/this company will
compensate in full within the limits of/the policy.
    It is most important that you let me/know if you do in
fact intend to proceed as/I have suggested, and that you
inform me of the/outcome.
    Yours faithfully,   (193)

Letter B

To: Sales Manager, Dutch Bulb Company, Spalding, Lincolnshire.

From: Andrew Anderson, 15/Greenfield Road, Glasgow.

Dear Sir,

I read your advertisement in/this week's "Sunday Times" and I would like to order/100 Gold Harvest daffodils, 100 Metropolitan tulips, one/dozen of your latest hybrid tea-rose, New York, and/one dozen assorted rose bushes which you have specially selected/for their rich fragrance.

I have just moved to this/property where the soil appears to be good and I/look forward to better results than I was able to/achieve in my previous garden, which resulted in my complete/abandonment of gardening as a hobby.

Although it is now/September, I understand that the roses will not be delivered/until November. On the other hand the bulbs should be/planted without too much delay and no doubt you will/be despatching them within the course of the next few/days.

My cheque for the total cost of the order,/plus postage, is enclosed.

Yours faithfully,   (166)

Unit E—Technique

How to Drill

After reading through an exercise, copy it into your notebook leaving two or three blank lines below each line of shorthand. Avoid drawing outlines; copy quickly and accurately, saying the words to yourself as you write. Fill the blank lines from subsequent dictation.

Write out a line of different outlines (12-14 each line) and then complete that page line by line, saying the word(s) to yourself as you write.

When certain outlines prove difficult to absorb, write a full line of one outline and then go on to complete a half page or page of that same outline until you feel that it has been mastered.

To get the hand moving quickly, complete a line with joined letter 'o' in longhand style; write rapidly and complete the page. Vary this technique by sometimes having widely spaced letters and at other times keeping them closely spaced.

Write a continuous line of the joined letters 'h' and 'y'. Turn the book upside down and you should still be able to read a line of joined 'hy'—if you are writing accurately. Improvement in this work will help your shorthand style.

Compose drills to meet your own specific needs. Concentrate on short forms, intersections and phrases.

118

CHAPTER 11

Unit A—Short Forms and Derivatives

Drill the following:

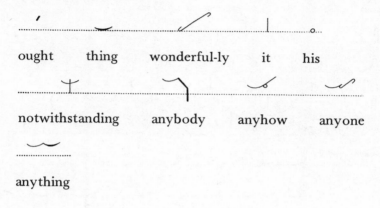

ought   thing   wonderful-ly   it   his

notwithstanding   anybody   anyhow   anyone

anything

1. Read through the following passage, noting how long it takes you. If you cannot read any outline check the key.

Time . . . . . . mins . . . . . . secs

2. Repeat the reading exercise, aiming to increase your reading speed. Note your timing.

Time . . . . . . mins . . . . . . secs

3. Drill all outlines which caused you any hesitancy in the last reading. Now repeat the reading, aiming to read the shorthand as quickly as if the material was typewritten. This final reading should be followed by dictation of the passage.

Time . . . . . . mins . . . . . . secs

119

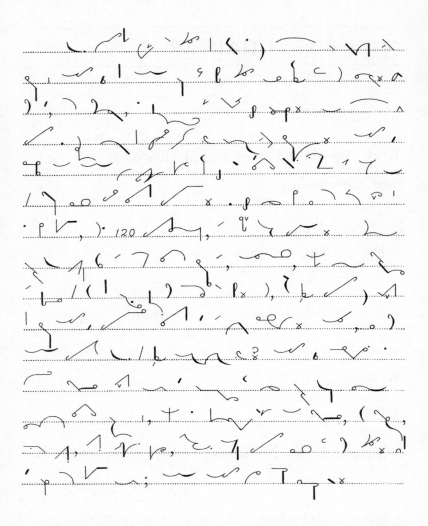

Having learned the theory of shorthand it ought to be/an easy matter to build up speed but anyone who/has had anything to do with the study of shorthand/knows that it is not quite so simple. First of/all there ought, or there must be, a determination on/the part of the student to succeed. No matter how/ wonderful the system may be it still requires real effort/to move up the speed ladder. Anyone who succeeds in/anything will usually tell you that it did not all/happen by magic and the only thing which brought success/was hard work. The student must set his or her/mind on a set target, say 120/ words a minute, and strive for that one thing. So/many people have reached this and much higher speeds and,/in some cases, notwithstanding the many problems and difficulties which/ they had to face during their course of study. So,/although it is not wonderfully easy to write at speed/anyone who works hard ought and will be successful. Anyhow,/is there anything worth having which does not involve effort?/Anyone who is experiencing a lack of progress right now/ought to keep in mind that most people have had/something similar happen to them but, notwithstanding a temporary halt/in progress, they persevered, kept reading, writing and drilling outlines,/and finally enjoyed wonderful success with their shorthand. You ought/to set your target now; anything anyone else can do/ you can do too. (244)

Unit B—Phrasing

Intersections (II) — R(down) arrange-d-ment — R(down) dot ing arranging — Bs business — Th month — R(up) require-d-ment — KR corporation.

1. Read through the shorthand passage, noting how long it takes you. If you cannot read any outline encircle it in pencil and check it in the key.

Time . . . . . . mins . . . . . . secs

2. Drill all outlines encircled in pencil. Repeat the reading, aiming for an increased reading speed.

Time . . . . . . mins . . . . . . secs

3. Make a fair copy of the passage in your own notebook. Look at the shorthand material, absorb several outlines and then make your own notes without reference to the printed passage. At first you might be able to recall only one complete outline to transfer to your own notes, but with practice you will be able to write several outlines, or a short sentence, without referring to the passage.

4. Now a final reading before receiving the passage from dictation. The aim is to read RAPIDLY.

A large corporation is often an international company with offices/and factories in all parts of the world. On the/other hand a corporation may be the title of one/of the many local authorities in a country, which would/mean that it is quite a small business involved in/running one particular local area. Large or small, these corporations/have to balance their books each month and they must/arrange to have their financial affairs in good order. It/is so easy for any business to go wrong, even/within one month, and therefore it is wise that the/Law sometimes does require financial details to be made available/to the public. A private corporation does not have to/meet such specific requirements but very often those responsible for/the running of that large business impose their own special/requirements. Such arrangements ensure the smooth running of their business./ (150)

Unit C—The Skill of Shorthand Writing

1. The following passage contains information about shorthand writing which should prove to be useful to you as a student shorthand writer. Read through the passage, referring to the key for assistance if necessary.

2. Repeat the reading, noting the time it takes and encircling in pencil any outline which causes hesitancy in reading.

> Time . . . . . . mins . . . . . . secs

3. Drill the outlines which caused hesitancy. How many times you drill is a very individual thing. Write the outline several, or many, times repeating it to yourself as you write, until you feel you have it under your control. Now make a final reading of the passage, noting your time, which should show a marked improvement on the first timing, in preparation for receiving the passage from dictation.

> Time . . . . . . mins . . . . . . secs

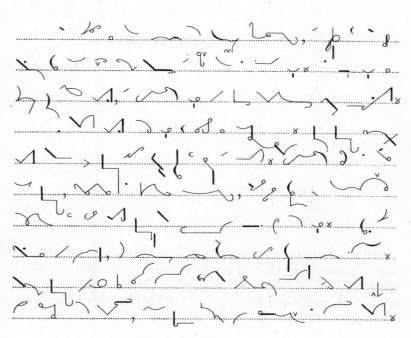

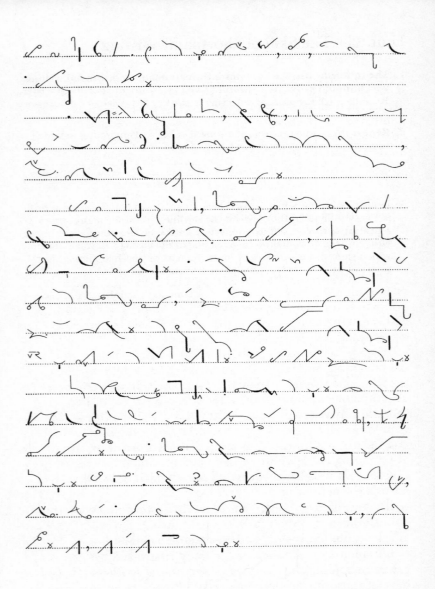

All shorthand is for immediate or eventual transcription, and it/is suggested that all students bear this in mind from/ the beginning and strive for an accurate note. A good/note is so much easier and faster to read, and/whenever notes are taken perfection should be the keyword.

The/ability to read your own notes without hesitation is indispensable./During dictation you may be required to read back to/the dictator and one ought to be able to do/this with speed and accuracy. Whenever there is a pause/in the dictation, perhaps a telephone interruption, always use this/time to familiarize yourself with what has already been dictated/by quickly going through your notes. These short breaks are/ limited, so make the most of them when they do/come along. Before the dictation recommences it is highly likely/that you will be respectfully called upon to read out/the last sentence or paragraph, and any difficulty on your/part will signify a lack of ability. Once you have/tried this checking through of your notes you will find/that you are, as a result, more productive and have/a wonderful confidence in your shorthand.

The build-up of/this confidence takes time, possibly several months, but if you/enter into the spirit of the thing you will find/there is a definite improvement over your earlier performance, and/finally you will have all you had ever wished for/in the skill.

When you get down to thinking about/it, transcription is the enormous bill which every business organization/pays for when employing a secretarial worker, and at times/it is questionable whether good value is received. An employer's/ valuation of you will be determined by what he thinks/of your transcription skill, and to him that means how/quickly you return dictation to him in mailable form. Your/speed of preparing mailable work will be determined by the/kind of note you write and your ability to read/it. Always one returns to the matter of your note./

At your earliest convenience get down to doing something about/your note. Most professional journals have advertisements for staff and/to meet the demanding requirements of our society accuracy is/stressed, notwithstanding the shortage of secretarial workers. If you have/a transcription problem make immediate arrangements to get to work/on your note. What is causing the problem? Some daily/application correcting faulty theory, revising short forms and a real/effort to familiarize yourself with your own note, will produce/results. Read, read, and read again your own notes.

(429)

125

Unit D—Correspondence

1. Read through the following two passages, referring to the key if necessary. Note carefully the outlines for towns and countries which may be new to you.

2. Drill any outlines new to you. Make a fair copy of each letter. Repeat the reading of each letter, noting the time.

> Time . . . . . . mins . . . . . . secs

3. Finally, repeat the reading. Aim to read *at least* 30 to 40 words a minute faster than your writing speed, which means that everyone should be reading at a rate of at least 100 words a minute. Note the time taken.

> Time . . . . . . mins . . . . . . secs

Letter A

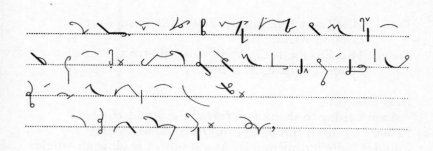

Letter B

To: Miss Janet Job, Editor, 2000, 128 Long Acre,
        London WC2E 9AN
From: Miss Elizabeth/Clark, 40 Gordon Street, Port of
        Spain, Trinidad, West Indies/

Dear Miss Job,
    I am writing to thank you for/all the wonderful help
"2000" has been throughout my/secretarial training. I
found it quite indispensable. As a result/of reading an article
in "2000" a short time/ago I have now decided to become
a medical secretary./
    Unfortunately I loaned that particular copy of "2000"
to/a friend and she has lost it. I wonder, therefore,/if you
would be good enough to supply me with/another copy so
that I can once again familiarize myself/with the training that is
necessary for me to become/a medical secretary.
    From the beginning of my shorthand studies/I enjoyed
the challenge of the subject and I have/tried my best
throughout my training. Whenever it has been/possible I
have taken down speeches and discussions at various/societies
and meetings and have helped my father in his/business.
    Your assistance will be very much appreciated.
    Yours sincerely,/   (190)

Letter B

To: Box Office Manager, Royal Festival Hall, South
        Bank, London S/E1
From: Miss Victoria Lee, 18 Fairway Grove, Aberdeen.

Dear/Sir,
    Please let me have at your earliest convenience a/copy of
the winter concert programme. I am the secretary/of our local
music society and your programme has been/indispensable
in past years in the planning of visits for/our members. I
know that early applications for seats are/essential and as
soon as I receive the latest programme/I will make
arrangements for the first visit of the/season.

I usually make a number of quite large bookings/each season and I wonder if there has been any/development in the idea of discounts for such bookings, or/for members of a recognized music society? Such discounts would/ certainly encourage our members to attend even more frequently because/any reduction would help to combat the ever-increasing cost/of travel from Scotland to London.

May I take this/opportunity of wishing you yet another highly successful season.

Yours/faithfully, (171)

CHAPTER 12

Unit A—Short Forms and Derivatives

Drill the following:

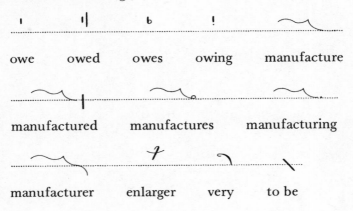

owe   owed   owes   owing   manufacture

manufactured   manufactures   manufacturing

manufacturer   enlarger   very   to be

1. Read through the following passage, noting how long it takes you.
   If you cannot read any outline check the key.

   Time . . . . . . mins . . . . . . secs

2. Repeat the reading exercise, aiming to increase your reading speed.
   Note your timing.

   Time . . . . . . mins . . . . . . secs

3. Drill all outlines which caused you any hesitancy in the last reading.
   Now repeat the reading, aiming to read the shorthand as quickly as
   if the material was typewritten. This final reading should be
   followed by dictation of the passage.

   Time . . . . . . mins . . . . . . secs

130

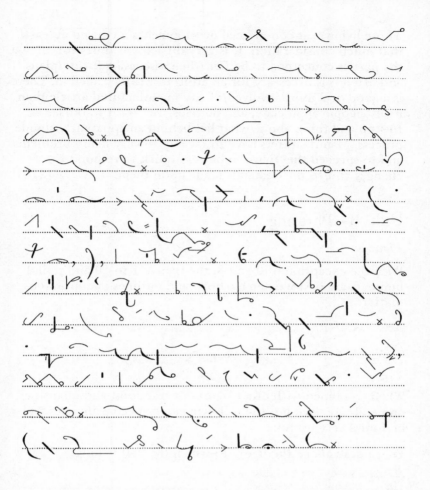

To be successful a manufacturer must always be looking for/ new markets where the products can be sold and for/new products to manufacture. Expansion in the manufacturing world is/very common and a company owes it to the employees/ to expand whenever possible. This will bring more work into/ the area and greater prosperity to the manufacturer and his/ staff. As an enlarger of factory premises the owner also/must owe something to the people not employed by the/company but who live nearby. They have a right to/be protected from over-development. Anyone who can be described/as a commer- cial enlarger must, therefore, take notice of local/requirements.

Those living near commercial developments are owed at least/ that much consideration. It is very difficult at times for/all the parties concerned to be fair when discussing future/plans and often it is necessary for an arbitrator to/be called in. There is a good deal more involved/in any manufactured article than many people appreciate, and perhaps/we owe it to ourselves to stop and think about/what lies behind an apparently simple process. Manufacturers have to face up to very many problems, and to succeed they/have to be very quick to respond to changes and/to the demands made upon them. (216)

Unit B—Phrasing

Figures

With the exception of 0 and 8, the figures 1 to 10 and round numbers are best written as shorthand outlines in continuous matter:

When combined with other figures or fractions, and quantities, numerals are used but the following high-speed principles will be found very useful:

½ — a dash *above* the figure to which the half belongs

1̄	2̄	3̄
1½	2½	3½%

¼ — a dash with an initial tick *above* the figure

3	4
3¼	4¼%

¾ — a dash with a final tick

7	8
7¾	8¾%

hundred — stroke 'n' under the figure

1	2
100	200

132

thousand — 'Th' after the figure

10(*7(56*   *10(9*

10,000   7,056   10,900

million — stroke 'm' under the figure

9   *9 273(6*

9,000,000   9,273,006

For decimalized figures use the dot for "point"

5.75   *9.25*

5.75%   9.25

Use the shorthand outline for "pounds"

17.ₓ34   *10.ₓ50*

£17.34   £10.50

Now drill all these short cuts with a large variety of figure combinations. Drill and master each new principle.

Unit C—The Skill of Shorthand Writing

1. The following passage contains information about shorthand writing which should prove to be useful to you as a student shorthand writer. Read through the passage, referring to the key for assistance if necessary.

2. Repeat the reading, noting the time it takes and encircling in pencil any outline which causes hesitancy in reading.

Time . . . . . . mins . . . . . . secs

3. Drill the outlines which caused hesitancy. How many times you drill is a very individual thing. Write the outline several, or many, times repeating it to yourself as you write, until you feel you have it under your control. Now make a final reading of the passage, noting your time, which should show a marked improvement on the first timing, in preparation for receiving the passage from dictation.

Time . . . . . . mins . . . . . . secs

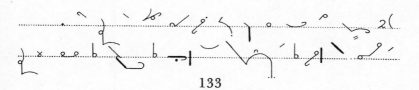

134

The particular system of shorthand you are using here today/ is known as the Pitman 2000 system. Since its/publication it has gained in popularity and it is used/by secretaries and shorthand-typists in various parts of the/world. Many people may also learn the system and then/use it purely as a personal skill in their various/walks of life — engineers, doctors, lawyers, and literally thousands of/others. Once learned, most people find they never forget Pitman's/Shorthand, although they may not use it regularly, and it/has proved to be an immensely useful skill.

Pitman/2000 Shorthand can cope with the ever-changing demands of/the modern business world. It has the speed potential to/allow the writer to take dictation with absolute confidence from/any dictator in any line of trade, manufacture or profession./We owe it to the system to write shorthand notes/that will live up to the fine reputation already established./

In the prospectus of most colleges you will find Pitman's/ Shorthand offered as a subject for study. Any student leaving/ such a course with a good shorthand skill and general/secretarial training will seldom experience difficulty in obtaining a good/job in any part of the world. Employers over the/years have come to appreciate what a fine skill shorthand/is, and most do inquire whether or not you do/have a certificate for Pitman's Shorthand. You might well wonder/if there is anything else. Surprisingly there are many other/systems on the market today — British, American, continental, manual (pen/ and pencil) and machine. (264)

Unit D—Correspondence

1. Read through the following two passages, referring to the key if necessary. Note carefully the outlines for towns and countries which may be new to you.

2. Drill any outlines new to you. Make a fair copy of each letter. Repeat the reading of each letter, noting the time.

Time . . . . . . mins . . . . . . secs

3. Finally, repeat the reading. Aim to read *at least* 30 to 40 words a minute faster than your writing speed, which means that everyone should be reading at a rate of at least 100 words a minute. Note the time taken.

Time . . . . . . mins . . . . . . secs

Letter A

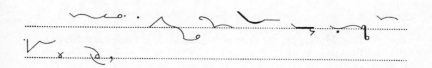

Letter B

Letter A

To: The Manager, New Look Limited, 9 Carnaby Street,
        London W/1
From: Miss Jane Robinson, 27 Richmond Street, Calgary,
        Alberta,/Canada.

Dear Sir,

A recent advertisement in the Clothing Manufacturers'/
Journal came to my attention and I am writing to/inquire
further about representing your company as well as selling/
your range of goods in this country.

I have been/in business at my present address for 4½/years.
Whilst I cannot give you precise trading figures/at this stage
of negotiations I can say that my/annual turnover is in excess
of the equivalent of/£30,000; profit percentages vary between
12½%,/the very lowest, to 50%.

I have seen/some of the lines you manufacture and I
would be/very interested in selling your goods and acting
as your/representative in Alberta. I feel sure such a project
would/be to our mutual benefit. I have a very well-/organized
business.

I am enclosing a reference from my bank/together with
the name and address of my attorney.

Yours/faithfully,   (181)

Letter B

To: Managing Director, Central Airways Limited, 93
        Baker Street, London/W1
From: Bernard Taylor, 32 Grant Road, Dublin, Ireland./

Dear Sir,

I am organizing a trip to the United/States for a group of
students from my college. I/understand that there is a
projected scheme for students travelling/between New York
and London costing £40. I appreciate/that should this be
agreed upon between the airlines such/a fare will be subject
to Government approval. I further/understand that it is

proposed to offer a discount of/7½% on block bookings made at/least 4 months in advance; this involves a certain percentage/of the fare not being returned in the event of/the passenger cancelling.

Since there has been no official publication/whatever about these fares from the airlines, or your Ministry/of Transport, I wonder if you could let me have/your comments on the present situation and the projected changes/in the immediate future? I cannot give you any more/details of our plans other than that there will be/at least 25 in the party and that we/shall be travelling in July.

Yours faithfully,

(197)